BLUEGRASS

BLUEGRASS

From the lonesome wail of a mountain
love song to the hammering drive
of the Scruggs-style banjo –
the story of an American
musical tradition

Bob Artis

HAWTHORN BOOKS, INC.
PUBLISHERS/New York

BLUEGRASS

Library of Congress Catalog Card Number: 74-33588
ISBN: 0-8015-0758-8
 2 3 4 5 6 7 8 9 10

This book is
very much a collaboration.
I dedicate it
to my collaborator,
Karen Artis.

Contents

Preface

Fifteen years have passed since I heard my first bluegrass record and laid my hands on a Gibson *A* model mandolin. Before I could drive a car I would walk miles to the nearest record store in search of any LP with the word *bluegrass* on it. Los Angeles wasn't the world's bluegrass Mecca, but most of the records made the rounds there before going out of print. I could kick myself whenever I think of the rare records, now high-priced collector's items, that I passed over because the names of the artists were unfamiliar to me.

Bluegrass has come a long way since then, and I guess I have, too. Raised on the music of Spade Cooley, Hank Thompson, and the Maddox Brothers and Rose, I was weaned from country music to rock in the mid-1950s (probably in search of roots) and finally to bluegrass. Bluegrass must have been the most satisfying, because that's where I've been ever since.

This book is about that music—the music that pierced the soul of a fourteen-year-old Californian. I honestly can't describe what bluegrass did to me the first time I heard it. It didn't have to grow on me; it stirred something inside me that I hardly knew was there. Whatever it was, I still haven't recovered. The Stanley Brothers and Bill Monroe can still make the hair on the back of my neck stand up like spring cattails.

I consider myself extremely fortunate to have received my bluegrass education before the current bluegrass "revival." That's partly what this book is about. It's also the story of bluegrass itself, which too few people know.

PREFACE

Mitch Jayne, noted comic bassist for the Dillards rock-bluegrass band, once wrote a stirring piece for *Muleskinner News*. He tells of seeing Bill Monroe on the TV show "To Tell the Truth." Bill Monroe, the father of a complete, dynamic chapter in American music. Bill Monroe, the legendary, living father of a worldwide music movement. The Kitty Carlisles and Bill Cullenses not only failed to recognize the man, but they'd never even heard of him or his music. That's also part of what this book is about.

This book has no revelations for those who have followed bluegrass. It doesn't expound any new or revolutionary theories. I haven't tried to come up with more neat old photographs than anybody else. What I have tried to do is tell the story of bluegrass in the most direct and logical way possible. Admittedly, I have glossed over parts of it for the sake of clarity. (*You* try relating the entire history of country music in one chapter!) I've tried to untangle some of the knots and present a clear picture of what went on in country music's other world from 1940 to the present. The necessary information is here. I'll leave the minute esoterica to others. It is my hope that this book will offer a little welcome perspective in an age in which many bluegrass artists have lost contact with the roots and in which the new kids coming up don't know Pee Wee Lambert from a Lambretta.

Musicians in other fields of music often wonder why country musicians never bother to learn to read music. It has little to do with literacy, more to do with the differences between oral traditions and written ones. The country people have always favored the former. With bluegrass musicians, it has more to do with the improvisational character of the music and the inability to come up with an adequate musical symbol for "soul."

Most of us in bluegrass have learned our music by listening to it. It's simply impossible to fully understand the style without getting a good, strong dose of it. It is suggested that the reader "listen" to this book while reading it, or having read it, that he go back and listen to some of the songs mentioned throughout. In the Appendix I've listed a few of the records that will make listening a little easier and what I've written a lot clearer. For example, one listening to the Stanley Brothers' "Mother No Longer Awaits Me at Home" on Starday will probably tell you more about them and their music than a hundred chapters.

Bluegrass, for better or worse, is changing every year. I expect a lot of what I write will be obsolete in a few years. But if this book leads just one young person to bum a scratchy copy of Flatt and Scruggs' "Foggy Mountain Jamboree" from someone, and if that young person is as stunned

PREFACE

by the experience as I was fifteen years ago, I will feel this work is justified. And, hopefully, when he treks miles to the record store in hopes of finding an ancient copy of that first Reno and Smiley gospel King LP, he won't, in his ignorance, pass over Red Ellis and Jimmy Williams on Starday.

Acknowledgments

There are many who deserve sincere thanks for making this book possible. I would like to express my appreciation to Peter Greenwood for bringing this project to my attention and to my editor, Sandra Choron, for her guidance and enthusiasm throughout.

Thanks also to *Bluegrass Unlimited* and *Muleskinner News* for making their resources available to me, and to their respective editors, Pete Kuykendall and Fred Bartenstein, for having taken time to discuss content, direction, and ideas on this book and on the state of the art in general. Thanks also to Lew Scheinman, Paul Gerry, Mark Yacavone, Gene Yellin, and others too numerous to mention for their kind advice and assistance.

My deepest gratitude goes to those who helped me with the mechanics of writing and photography: Jim Vallela, for patiently editing and proofreading the mountains of copy and offering invaluable professional advice; Ted Washabaugh, for converting an odds and ends assortment of photographic material into a set of superior black and white prints; and my inhumanly patient, energetic, and understanding wife, Karen, for helping me with every phase of this book.

I also must express my heartfelt thanks to the legion of musicians who have given bluegrass the spark of genius.

Introduction

Old-time bluegrass musicians notice it more and more lately, especially in the past few years since the theme from the movie *Deliverance* became popular. Young faces in the audience, beaming up at them, giving them a little of the recognition and approval that the country music industry has denied them for the past two or three decades. Flatt and Scruggs went to Japan and received the adulation once reserved for the likes of the Beatles. The *New York Times* reported that the Easter weekend old-time fiddlers' convention at Union Grove, North Carolina, drew crowds estimated at 100,000. Bill Monroe, the "father of bluegrass," has been quoted as saying, "The college kids are my best audience. They know when you're playing it right."

Bluegrass pours from every television and radio. There was "The Beverly Hillbillies" TV show (and later "Hee Haw") for those so inclined. And there was *Bonnie and Clyde*, and, of course, *Deliverance*. Then there are those scores of commercials in which the banjo tinkles in the background or blasts in the foreground tempting us to buy certain brands of toothpaste, cornflakes, apple wine, or airline tickets. You can't get through a day without hearing at least *some* bluegrass music. But after all the ballyhoo, the man on the street still doesn't seem to know that something very special is happening.

That word keeps popping up. *Bluegrass*. Who knows what it is exactly? Veteran Rolling Stones bassist Bill Wyman says he wants to get into more bluegrass. Does that mean he wants to take up the banjo and start learning Bill Monroe songs? Hardly. He probably means he wants to do more of the funky, down-home things (less slick and more gutsy than Nashville pop-country) that a lot of people mistake for bluegrass.

Bluegrass is a specific. It was given the name because it was something distinctly different from pop-country, electric hillbilly, or any other kind of country music.

The average consumer doesn't know that most top-forty country radio stations won't program bluegrass—even on a bribe. It's good enough to sell toothpaste or cornflakes, but in this age when country music seems to be at its zenith, the powers in Nashville consider bluegrass—of all things—"too country."

Volumes have been turned out on the history of what Nashville considered its music, and one or two of them might even have a chapter (seldom two chapters) on bluegrass. But generally, there never has been a place to turn if you want to learn even a little about this growing and very important slice of American music. The card catalog and reader's guide at the library will offer little or nothing under the heading "Bluegrass." You will probably be directed to look under "Country Music," and there will be precious little about bluegrass there. The record store won't be much help either. Most record outlets won't stock bluegrass records because they're not fast-moving items. Yet the same stores will stock equally slow-moving jazz and classical records because somewhere along the line those forms have acquired the aridly respectable title and status of "art."

Classic-traditional bluegrass music surely isn't the stuff that graces the top-ten charts. It's mountain music, and only the mountain people and those others sensitive enough to grasp the feelings of the country people and their hard, poverty-bred realities can fully appreciate the simple, eloquent songs of death and lost lovers, lonesome mountains and deep religious faith, cabin homes on hills and gray-haired parents awaiting the return of the wandering boy. The high, haunting sound of a tenor-range trio, the hammering drive of the Scruggs-style banjo, and the lonesome wail of a fiddle have an appeal that goes beyond region and background, beyond music prejudice and cultural differences, beyond the hard categories of "urban" and "rural." It's more than the music of one people and their way of life. The instrumentation is dazzling and the ring of the banjo captivating, and a whole new generation has discovered in bluegrass the most honest, forthright statement of human emotions to be found.

Bluegrass seems as old as the hills themselves. It isn't. Kentuckian Bill

INTRODUCTION

Monroe forged a personal style of tradition-based mountain string music that drew heavily from the older styles, almost as a reaction to the many negative things happening to country music in the 1940s. The slick vocalists and electric guitars were just straying too far from the roots, and Monroe brought it all back home, wrapped in a new and exciting package. The extent to which he succeeded may be seen in the thousands who camp for a week at a time in the rutted pastures of the big bluegrass festivals just to be close to it, to play it, sing it, live it, and be a part of it. The Bill Monroe impact may be seen and heard in dozens of bands, hundreds perhaps, who have followed his example since the mid-1940s and have stayed true to the pure, unamplified sounds of the banjo, fiddle, mandolin, flat-top guitar, dobro, and upright bass. When you talk to them about their music, don't call it country. And please don't call it country and western. Call it bluegrass.

Today there is a movement finally coming up from that nebulous netherworld referred to as underground. The thousands who throng to the festivals in the warmer months have proved, especially to the skeptical businessmen in Nashville, that there is indeed a hard-cash market for the pure stuff. Bluegrass used to be associated with hayseed comedians. Now many consider it the intellectual side of country music. Open-minded, well-adjusted, secure people are finding that you don't have to be the moronic result of two centuries of Appalachian inbreeding to appreciate, admire, and even genuinely love bluegrass music.

Bluegrass has taken so many varied and surprising directions in recent years that it may be in danger of losing touch with its own roots, just as country music did in the 1940s and 1950s, but that's hardly the point. The point is that thousands of people, many of them the young of the urban North, have adopted bluegrass as their own. Its candidness and instrumental brilliance say something significant that they want to hear, something they can't find in any other music style. Only bluegrass has the open earthiness of the country and the sophistication of technical virtuosity in exactly the right proportions.

There is a great desire today to get back to the genuine human values, to return to the soil, and to find roots in today's most common form of artistic expression—music. Bluegrass celebrates the earth and the basic human condition in a way that is both direct and musically valid. It's a healthy and predictable reaction to the super-cynical age of future-shock and Alice Cooper.

BLUEGRASS

1

Mountains and Music

THE ROOTS

Volumes have been written on the history of country music, but very little specifically on the history of bluegrass. The history of one, up to about 1940, is a history of the other; they are two branches of the same very old and distinguished tree.

It doesn't take an especially well-trained ear to tell that bluegrass has more roots intact than does the current product manufactured for mass consumption at the country music capital in Nashville. After several years' absence the fiddle is again in vogue in pop-country circles. It never left bluegrass. Neither did the mandolin or five-string banjo. Bluegrass smoothed the squeaks out of the fiddle and brought the banjo out of the nineteenth century. It isn't "old-time" anymore, but if the music brought from the British Isles by the first white settlers has a modern heir, it's bluegrass and not modern "country."

Music has been in the hills as long as people have been there. Some of the songs sung today as part of the standard bluegrass song bag could have been heard over two centuries ago, drifting through the mountains from the backs of creaking, ox-drawn wagons, out of cabin windows and log church houses. Many of them were rediscovered as folk songs several years ago, but most of the older bluegrass artists learned them from their parents, who learned them from *their* parents, and so on back through the dim and misty past of the dark, mossy hollows of central Appalachia.

The accents were once tinged with British and Scotch-Irish inflection, but eventually the slow life of the remote southern highlands melted speech into a drawl resembling that of their neighbors of the southern flatlands. Their traditions and music evolved into a personality and sound as uniquely mountain as it had once been British.

Life in Appalachia is hard even today, and we can imagine what it must have been like a century or two ago. In most places the land is not good. The eastern and western slopes of the wide mountain chain are flat and rolling enough for cotton and cattle and corn and tobacco, but the central mountain soil is often rocky and unyielding, and the mountainsides are too steep to plow. *Living* often meant squeezing a bare-survival crop of corn from a mountaintop or valley-bottom dirt farm and keeping a few scrawny milk cows. There was some trapping, and logging provided work until most of the trees were gone and the mills shut down. Then, early in the twentieth century, the coal companies came, gouging and scarring the hills and ridges to feed the progress that was settling everywhere but in the mountains. Mining brought jobs and a new set of hazards: labor riots, cave-ins, and a disease called black lung.

My own grandfather, Frank Dunn, was a coal miner from a little place called Coal Hill, Arkansas. He earned a good wage before World War I by going into new shafts, carbide lamp and kerosene lantern ablaze, checking for leaking gas. If gas was present, the flame of his lantern would ignite it and probably burn him to death. My grandmother, who was from Russellville, dreamed one night that he was carried home on a stretcher, badly burned. She was awakened by a knock at the door. It was one of his fellow miners; the nightmare had come true. A similar story is told in a bluegrass song, a tune from the older traditions called "Dream of the Miner's Child." Carter Stanley, one of the Stanley Brothers, sang the song. He, too, was once a coal miner.

But even after the coal companies came and some of the towns grew into cities, for many it was still an isolated life in a world where the sound of a neighbor's ax ringing up the hollow meant that civilization was moving in. The curl of wood smoke from another man's chimney and the crowing of a rooster other than one's own were things seldom experienced. Medicine was homemade, and each winter brought hunger and sickness and death. It was a limited world, with God and the family at its center; and the basic, hard realities of mountain life created attitudes that were the mountain man's own.

MOUNTAINS AND MUSIC

Music was as much a part of life in the New World as it had been in the old. There were the old Protestant hymns and the ballads, and there was the highly ornamented fiddle music that the people danced to at weddings and corn-huskings. It was playful music, and the fiddle tunes, like the ballads and the hymns, were passed from father to son in an endless handing down of the musical traditions. Many of the old fiddle tunes—songs like "Devil's Dream" and "Billy in the Low Ground"—are also still a vital part of today's bluegrass.

The tradition of the fiddler still lives in most rural areas, in the mountains and elsewhere. It takes years to become a good fiddler; not everyone can cut it, and a good fiddler is something special. Technique as well as tradition have to be well within the fiddler's grasp, and those fifteen- and twenty-minute cake walks at the end of a night's square dancing are as physically demanding as pitching an inning of major-league baseball. While most square-dance callers today prefer to play records—they're consistent and cheaper than paying live musicians—an accomplished fiddler is still in demand and is becoming too scarce to suit a lot of people.

In the beginning there were regional fiddle styles, all within the limits of the tradition: In New England and Canada the sound of the pipes and fiddling of the British Isles were retained, while the music of the southern mountains developed a droning, sad sound. Isolated from outside influences in the rugged, solitary ridges and hollows of Kentucky, east Tennessee, and Virginia, most of what the mountain man knew of the world around him was what he could see with his own eyes and what he had been taught by previous generations. Changes had to come gradually and from within, and in time his music acquired a sound as lonesome, rough, and honest as the people whose lives it reflected.

If there was a primary folk instrument, it was the fiddle. There were dulcimers, too, both the multi-stringed type based on the Hungarian cymbalom and the elongated northern European type popularized by Jean Ritchie. The dulcimers weren't widely used though; they could be popular in one hollow but virtually unknown in the surrounding area. The fiddle seemed more versatile and structurally durable, and thus easier to carry from place to place. It was the fiddle of the classic Italian shape and design that survived the changes of time in the mountains, as it did elsewhere.

Something new was added in the middle of the nineteenth century—the banjo. In the 1840s someone took the crude version, with its varying number of strings, standardized it, made it manufacturable, and arrived at a set number of strings. For the next half-century all banjos had five strings; four running the length of the instrument and a short, high-pitched fifth string running only halfway up the neck. A white minstrel named Joel Sweeney took credit for the "invention," and it became something of a musical rage. The Civil War drew many young men out of the mountains to the battlefields of the south, and they brought the concept of the banjo back home with them. By the turn of the century the banjo was being widely manufactured and sold through the mail order houses, and it was becoming so common in the hills that a country band was thought of in terms of the fiddle and banjo.

Like the mountain fiddlers, the mountain banjo pickers developed their own personal and regional styles. There was not even any set way of tuning a banjo, let alone playing one, and many used the minstrel styles, while others experimented with the possibilities. A three-finger style is often associated with the Carolinas, while some Kentuckians used just the thumb and first finger. But most used a sort of controlled down-strum that has come to us as "frailing" or "clawhammer" style, much like that played rather raucously by country comedian Louis "Grandpa" Jones. Whatever style was used, the people of the rural South found the five-string banjo almost as good as the fiddle for accompanying their ballads.

The mail order houses, with their thick, goods-laden catalogs, were a boon to the country people, who bought many of their manufactured goods through the mail, as well as seeds for planting and the patent medicines guaranteed to cure croup, quinsy, swelled breasts, gout, cold hands, and dandruff. The catalog showed them what was going on in the world of fad and fashion, music and the arts. Part of the fashion trend of 1900 was toward things Latin, as immigrants from southern Europe poured into the big American cities. Mandolin ensembles were making the concert rounds, and cheap prints of the *Battleship Maine* and *The Charge Up San Juan Hill* graced almost every wall. And two new instruments appeared in the catalogs: the guitar and the mandolin.

The guitar had been popular in Europe in the late eighteenth century, but the mountain man didn't start exploring its possibilities until around 1900. When he finally discovered it, he found it better than the fiddle for accompanying his singing, better than the banjo for backing up a fiddle—and the combination of the three was just about unbeatable. The basic country string band formula had been found. It would change very little in the next half-century.

Progress was the key word as the new century bounded in. Changes were everywhere. Thousands poured into the mountains, digging coal, laying track, milling lumber. New railroads wound through the Blue Ridge and the Great Smokies, and electricity lit the streets of Galax, Virginia, and Hazard, Kentucky. New ideas were breaking the seal of a century of isolation and new gadgets were finding a welcome place in even the most remote dwelling. The cabin dweller must have been nothing less than astounded to hear the first cylinder recordings of Enrico Caruso and John Philip Sousa. It may have been viewed as a trivial novelty, but by 1920 the phonograph was sold through retail furniture outlets everywhere in the South.

Before technology began its fateful hike into the mountains, most music was confined to the hearth and home. After the day's work was done, the more musically inclined would sit around the fire or outside on the porch and sing. An old crone who was the mother of fifteen and called "aunt" by everyone for miles around would know several croaking verses of the song about "Fair Ellender," and the blind man rumored to be her son would play the fiddle while she sang, his keen ears following the chilling inflections of her voice. Back and forth the songs would go, each family member taking a turn. An old man, the brother of the old woman, would sing a song in the same style about Jonah being swallowed by the fish on his way to warn the citizens of Ninevah of God's wrath at their wickedness. There seemed to be almost no melody or chords, just a continuing wail, high and mournful, until the storyline reached its end.

Then the old man would play one on his fiddle, just music, mumbling something now and again about "Shake that little foot, Sally Ann," and everyone would rock a little faster in their chairs and tap their feet. The younger kids would dance barefoot in the dust in front of the porch until they were told that the dust was getting a little too thick up where the grown-ups were. Things would get going, and someone would tell one of the kids to run up the creek bed and get the neighbors; tell the old man up there to bring his banjo.

That was their music: homemade and for the home. The fiddler inherited his instrument and songs from his father, the old woman got her songs from her mother, and no one remembered where it all started. There could have been several musicians just a few miles away, but if the folks at this particular cabin had heard of them, they had probably never seen them. Their limited style, whatever it was, consisted entirely of what they inherited from those who came before them along with the very little they added to it themselves.

The phonograph changed things. It was a revelation; now they had something to listen to and learn from, something from which to draw new ideas, a whole world of music for just a few cents a disc. Now an evening's entertainment might well mean sitting around listening to the old wind-up Victrola. It wasn't long before the sounds of ragtime and Hawaiian music found their way into the record collections of the country people.

New ideas bring change, and the changes were evident in the music. The Hawaiian lap-guitar, popular on the vaudeville stage and disc recordings, began to appear in country bands that might otherwise have included only fiddle, guitar, and banjo. Country banjo pickers could now hear the "classical" banjo players of the Fred Van Eps school, and the old-time fiddlers could get a taste of what the violin was "supposed" to sound like.

Next came the radio. Mass communication saw no greater boon than the little box that talked. There were several hundred commercial radio stations broadcasting by the early 1920s, many of them in the South. A lot of the programming was done live in those days (almost all of it, in fact), and the radio stations didn't have to look far to find good local talent. Country music had been home music before, strictly an amateur enterprise, but now the rural fiddlers and balladeers had a chance to take their music to a larger audience, and perhaps even turn professional.

Country music was being widely broadcast by the mid-1920s. Even the most remote mountain cabin might have its battery set or crystal receiver. The neighbors would all come over on Saturday night and sit by the speaker listening to the big barn dance programs or the live broadcasts from stations like Atlanta's WSB or WSM in Nashville. These and other early southern radio stations not only brought country music to a much wider audience, both North and South, but also brought the sounds of popular music and jazz into the lives of the country people. The mixing of musical ideas was bound to have an effect on the musical attitudes of both worlds.

It was just a matter of time before someone put the pieces together—the phonograph and the extensive radio play of country music—and decided that there might just be a market, however regional, for recordings of the rustic mountain sounds. As it happened, a recording company sales representative in Atlanta saw a flickering newsreel of a Georgia fiddlers' convention and was impressed not only by the size of the crowd but also by the audience's response to one of the fiddlers, a mountain man named "Fiddlin'" John Carson. The Okeh Recording Company dispatched Ralph Peer to investigate.

The man Peer met in Atlanta in the spring of 1923 was as rough and crude

8

as the moonshine he often bragged about making. Peer found Carson's old-time fiddling, untrained mountain voice, and generally uncouth ways a little distasteful at first and reportedly had trouble convincing his company that the fiddler could sell records. But they released the material, and much to everyone's surprise, it sold well in the mountains.

"Fiddlin' " John Carson was the first. Carson, Peer, and Okeh had proved the stuff would sell if pushed on the right market, and Peer's shrewd evaluation of what the mountain people wanted to hear gained him a place as one of the great pioneers in the American popular music industry. With the successes of the Carson releases, his good judgment was established and Okeh was quick to release a test-pressing by another mountain artist whose work they had passed over earlier—guitarist Henry Whitter. The country recording boom was on.

The discovery and exploration of any new ground is exciting. A whole new field of music was opening up, and each year brought new discoveries and popular performers. There was healthy competition among the major recording companies to find good native talent whose music they could record, promote, and sell to the southern regional market. The big companies began organizing and equipping field recording expeditions and sending them south.

The way in which talent was located involved a beautifully simple and direct approach. People like Ralph Peer and Columbia's Frank Walker would simply go into an area and run an ad in the local newspaper. Down they would come from the mountains, one by one: the bands, fiddlers, and balladeers. They would be auditioned, sorted and selected, rehearsed and recorded. The luckiest would get their work pressed into wax and put into commercial circulation throughout the South. Stars were being born, and bands like Gid Tanner and the Skillet Lickers (from northern Georgia) and Charlie Poole's North Carolina Ramblers were becoming as well known in the southern mountains as Paul Whiteman and Ted Lewis were in the North.

To the folk purists the years between 1925 and 1935 were the Golden Years of country music. Much of what was being recorded for commercial release was authentic folk music, music that had been developing in its own environment for generations. The early country recordings, when viewed as a single body, certainly rank as one of the most extensive blocks of traditional folk music ever collected.

Things sped along as the market grew. Okeh and Victor were among the first labels in the breach with their recordings of the solitary fiddlers John Carson and Eck Robertson. Vocalion was recording Uncle Dave Macon, a jocular, rustic banjo player who was the first star of the Grand Ole Opry. Gennett and Brunswick jumped into the field, and so did Victor, the biggest label of the day. Victor did a lot to break the ice jam of inner-office prejudice against the rural sound when it gave country music its first national hit, the song "Wreck of the Old 97," performed by Vernon Dalhart (Marion Try Slaughter), a popular singer from Texas. Based on the Henry Whitter version of the same song, the Victor recording still ranks among the biggest-selling country hits, even though it was recorded back in 1924. Victor couldn't argue with the cash returns from "Old 97," and Ralph Peer was soon on their payroll.

Again, the march of technology brought the winds of change. It was inevitable that the country artists themselves would start looking toward one another's recordings as a means of picking up new techniques and learning new songs. Most country artists had limited repertoires and quickly absorbed songs like "Old 97" and other popular tunes into their song lists. The result was a more unified sound in country music. A mish-mash of individual family and local styles marked the earliest records. Now a single style emerged, smoother but still reflecting the soul of the rural South in its fiddles and folk-style melodies. Some called it hillbilly. Others preferred the less derogatory title of country music.

Ralph Peer made one of his trips to Tennessee in the summer of 1927 to do some of the recording that by then had become routine. He ran his ad in the Tennessee-Virginia border town of Bristol. One of the acts to audition was a sickly-looking Mississippian named Jimmie Rodgers. Another was a family named Carter.

Alvin P. Carter was a salesman on his rounds in Virginia when he met a pretty girl named Sara Dougherty. Legend states that she was playing the guitar and singing the old train-wreck tune "Engine 143" when he first saw her. They married and began to sing together. Sara was often visited by her cousin Maybelle Addington, who eventually married A. P. Carter's brother. A. P., Sara, and Maybelle sang while Sara strummed an autoharp and Maybelle played a distinctive lead guitar. They caught on in their local area and were persuaded into going to Bristol to audition for the man who made the records.

Their simple, home-style harmonies and enormous repertoire of great old songs caught the ear of the South like none before them. Carter's rich bass voice blended with his wife's moving and soulful lead, joined on the choruses by the sweet, tenor-range voice of Maybelle. Their sound was smoother and more professional than that of any of the groups before them, but it still had that warmth-of-the-hearth sound that struck a responsive chord in the hearts of the country people. They recorded hundreds of songs between 1927 and their final performance as a group in 1941: blues, cowboy songs, old murder ballads, gospel tunes, humorous numbers, love songs, and timeless folk ballads they collected and arranged to suit their uniquely warm trio style. Their vocal style laid much of the groundwork for bluegrass singing, which was just beginning to emerge as the Carters were making their exit. Their huge output wasn't limited to Victor's Bluebird folk sublabel, and today their versions of "Keep on the Sunny Side," "John Hardy," "Little Darlin' Pal of Mine," "Thinking Tonight of My Blue Eyes," "Will the Circle Be Unbroken," "Homestead on the Farm," and "Wildwood Flower" are among the essential country songs.

As the music of the Carters was being broadcast from Texas to the Carolinas, they were shifting the country music emphasis from the old-time, whoop-'em-up fiddle breakdowns to the actual singing of songs, and more importance was being placed on good singing and harmony arrangements. But paralelling their successful career was the skyrocketing star of Jimmie Rodgers, shifting the spotlight even farther away from the old fiddle bands to the concept of the country singing star.

Rodgers, "The Singing Brakeman," was probably more responsible than anyone for the "advancement" of early country music. The consumptive son of a Mississippi railroader, he grew up in freight yards all over the South and West. He learned his music from blacks and whites, cowboys and mountaineers, laborers and roustabouts, and the resulting personal style was something that went beyond region. He had a song for everyone, and everyone seemed to buy what he was selling.

More than any other country artist of his era, Jimmie Rodgers had a magic quality that made him something a little special, a "star." Charisma or magnetism, personality or pizzaz, Rodgers had it and the world loved him, especially a world torn by the Great Depression. He sang the "blue yodels" picked up from the black traditions. He sang the songs of bumming freight trains, of life on the western plains. When he died of tuberculosis in 1933, he had become the closest thing country music ever had to a "king," and immediately an heir was sought. The very fact that people in the business realized Rodgers had established the pattern of the single singing

11

star and wished to continue it marked a big step in the maturity of the country music industry and gave birth to the scores of country singing giants who followed. It was a step toward maturity, but it was also a step away from tradition.

The stock market had collapsed in the fall of 1929, and the Great Depression brought the age of the southern field recording expeditions to an abrupt halt. The nation was shaken, and no one suffered more than the country people. They didn't even have the cash for the basic needs of everyday life, let alone the luxury of phonograph records. Records were still being made and sold, but the companies were cautious with their money, sticking safely to the bands and sounds that had already established their sales potential: the Carters, Rodgers, and Charlie Poole—the giants.

If the recording industry was forced to take a few steps backward, then radio was elevated one or two notches during the years of economic panic. Phonograph records cost money, but after the initial price was paid for a radio set, all the music in the world could be had by simply turning a dial. Many stations were broadcasting country music, and the Saturday night airings of the "National Barndance" from WLS in Chicago and Nashville's "Grand Ole Opry" became the major events of the week for thousands of families across the East. Somehow, among the bread lines, Oklahoma dust storms, and "Brother, Can You Spare a Dime?" the Golden Age of Country Recordings became the Golden Age of Country Radio.

The "Opry" and "Barn Dance" were the biggest and best, but hundreds of smaller radio stations sent live country music out over the airways during the darkest days of the Depression. This provided the many hillbilly bands with a means of staying in the business through the grim years. Some of the most popular acts acquired sponsors like the famous Crazy Water Crystal people, who sold mineral crystals that were supposed to have a rejuvenating effect on those who used them. The sponsors could assure the bands air time during which they could announce their personal appearances, which in turn would insure them a big paid attendance at their live shows in the surrounding countryside. The best of the bands could get prime time, which in the country areas was either in the very early predawn hours, when the farmers were getting up, or during the noontime meal break, when the farmers were in from the fields and the factory workers were out in their cars with the radios turned on.

Thousands today still remember the old "farm time" programs, whether they were broadcast at noon or at five o'clock in the morning. The band would come on strong with a singing jingle bidding the listeners welcome and putting in a strong plug for the sponsor's product. A smooth-voiced announcer would then cut in, obviously trying to speak with something other than a southern accent, giving the listeners a formal "good morning" and introducing the bandleader. The leader, if he was a good one, generally knew his audience wanted to hear the real down-home stuff. There would be a couple of fast fiddle tunes, an old ballad or two, and a funny song from the band's resident comedian. Then the announcer would cut back in with a word from the sponsor and maybe a word or two about where the "friends and neighbors" out in radio land could see the boys in person, at this or that country schoolhouse or miner's hall. There might be a plug about how the "friends and neighbors" could contact the band if they wanted to book them for *their* schoolhouse show, giving the musicians prospects of one or two more jobs. Then would come a little more music and a sign-off—all in just fifteen minutes of air time. Shows of almost identical content would run all day and into the evening, with each band getting the same plug for their personal appearances. The best bands drew the crowds and consequently stayed in business while keeping themselves and their families fed and clothed.

The "Grand Ole Opry," at Nashville's radio station WSM, soon established itself as the country's leading showcase for traditional music. Chicago's "National Barn Dance" was probably more important in spreading country music to the audiences of the North and Midwest, but its general sound lacked the heavy Appalachian flavor that characterized the "Opry." George Hay, looking like a middle-aged Harold Lloyd and calling himself The Solemn Old Judge, was the guiding light of the "Opry." He would introduce the acts with a reverence that added a touch of respect to the proceedings, a respect and reverence not always adhered to by the likes of the rascally, gold-toothed Uncle Dave Macon. There were the McGee Brothers and the Crook Brothers and the Delmores in an endless parade of traditional songs and fiddle tunes. There was the diminutive black man named DeFord Bailey who could play some powerful harmonica and who was referred to, not too touchingly, as the official mascot of the "Opry." The program was a combination barn dance, vaudeville show, and revival, with its foot-stomping square-dance tunes, dialect comedians, and hymn singing. It wasn't too long after its inception in the 1920s that the "Opry" represented the end of the rainbow for musicians in the southern mountains.

BLUEGRASS

Country-style music continued to grow through the radio years, and the major country variety programs brought the best of the bands to the widest audience. These acts were copied and imitated by thousands of amateurs who were still back in the hills, clustered around their old Atwater-Kents. The popular bands were emulated and in some cases bested, and new sophistication was reached every year. Singing was getting a bigger and better place in the hearts of the listeners, due to the delightful singing of the Carter Family, the yodeling croon of Jimmie Rodgers, and the tongue-in-cheek hillbilly warblings of Vernon Dalhart. Gene Autry was serenading the Midwest, cowboy style, from the stage of the "National Barn Dance" as the old singing styles became more popular and more polished. Out of the 1930s came a new development in country singing, the ultimate for its time: the country duet.

There had been duet and trio singing in the hills before the 1930s, of course: Sara and Maybelle Carter were one of the best, even though A. P.'s bass voice often was prominent below them. But the male duets were really catching on, and one of the best of the early ones was the Delmore Brothers, Alton and Rabon. They were from Alabama, and their style was relaxed and smooth, their approach polished almost to the point of slickness. Today, listening to their records of the 1930s, they seem astoundingly modern and commercial for their time. Their harmony was soft and light, and it was "good" harmony: They didn't sing in unison as even some of the later bands did. They obviously worked hard at doing what they did with as much perfection as possible. They used two guitars, a standard six-string model and a four-string tenor guitar, and we can probably attribute the rising popularity of lead-guitar playing in country music in the 1930s to the Delmores, as well as to Maybelle Carter and Sam McGee of the McGee Brothers. There's no question that the Delmore Brothers, who remained popular up through the late 1940s, were instrumental in giving rise to a strong and flourishing school of country duets in the mid-1930s.

The Delmore Brothers had used the unique combination of two guitars, but the standard instrumentation of the acts that followed them was almost always the guitar and the mandolin. The Callahan Brothers were successful with this combination, as were Mac and Bob, the two blind musicians at WLS. Then came Karl and Harty, also at the Chicago station, the Blue Sky Boys, and the Monroe Brothers. The school was carried into the 1940s with the Bailes Brothers and the Bailey Brothers, and even into the 1950s with the

14

Bill Monroe, the father of bluegrass. (*Tom Henderson*)

The Bailey Brothers—Charlie and Danny— in front of the radio mike at WPTF, Raleigh, North Carolina, ca. 1950. The Baileys were essentially a traditional country duet who often fronted a full bluegrass band. Charlie's mandolin is the one Bob Osborne has played for years. The Osbornes were once Charlie's sidemen.

Jimmie Rodgers (*Courtesy of Tim Nesit*

This handbill announced the Stanley Brothers' first Columbia release of the late 1940s, "White Dove." (*Courtesy of Norman Azinger*)

Ralph Stanley with Keith Whitley, shortly after the death of Roy Lee Centers in 1974. The Stanley tradition is probably the most enduring in the spectrum of bluegrass music. Bassist is Jack Cooke of Norton, Virginia, a veteran of the Stanley and Monroe bands. (*Karen Artis*)

"Martha White Flour Time" at the WSM studios. The Martha White Mills and their sponsorship gave Flatt and Scruggs an economic edge over many other groups. The photo is from the earliest days at WSM. Left to right: Bobby Moore, Benny Martin, Curly Sechler, Lester Flatt, and Earl Scruggs.

The Foggy Mountain Boys. By the time this photo was taken in the late 1950s, they had added a dobro guitar, played by the greatest in the field, Buck Graves. Hidden are bassist Jake Tullock and fiddler Paul Warren. Curly Sechler stands to the far right. (*Paul Gerry*)

This was Lester Flatt's band of the early 1970s, back to the straight bluegrass he had been unable to play during the last years with Scruggs. Left to right: dobroist Mike Bailey, banjoist Haskell McCormick, Lester Flatt, Curly Sechler (partially hidden), and Johnny Johnson. (*Karen Artis*)

Don Reno (right) and Red Smiley (left) at their peak.

Ramona and Grandpa Jones. Louis M. Jones has been known as Grandpa since he was in his twenties. Many purists scoff at Jones' show-biz approach to tradition, but he remains a link between the new Nashville and the old-time styles. His wife is a fine fiddler and mandolinist as well as a guitarist. (*Henry Horenstein*)

The classic Reno and Smiley band on stage. From left: Mack Magaha, Reno, Smiley, and John Palmer. (*Paul Gerry*)

Reno and Smiley were almost as popular for their zany hillbilly comedy as for their music. From left: Jeff Dooly, Tater (Mac Magaha), Chicken Hotrod (Don Reno), Pansy Hotrod (Red Smiley), and Mutt Highpockets (John Palmer).

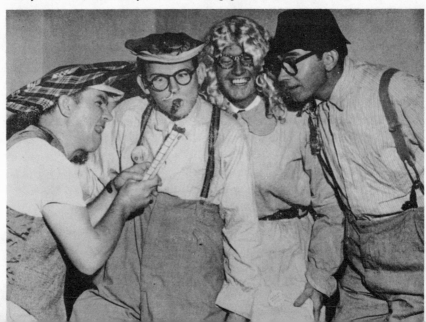

Jimmy Martin
(*Tom Henderson*)

Jimmy Martin and two of his Sunny Mountain Boys. Jimmy naturally mugs for the photographer. The mandolinist is Earl Taylor. (*Paul Gerry*)

Jim and Jesse and what may have been their finest band. Left to right: Bobby Thompson (standing), Don McHan, and Vassar Clements. Thompson and Clements are among the most sought-after session musicians in the country. McHan was the writer of many fine songs, including "Grave in the Valley," "I'll Wear the Banner," and "The Young Fisherwoman." Note the band's Western attire.

Jim and Jesse (or Jesse and Jim, in this case). The McReynolds Brothers combine Jesse's incredible mandolin playing with Jim's equally acclaimed tenor voice to make the most beautifully blended duet in the field. (*Ron Petronko*/Bluegrass Unlimited)

MOUNTAINS AND MUSIC

Louvin Brothers. But long before that, back in the mid-1930s, the tradition of the guitar-mandolin duet had become as firmly established as a part of country music as the old fiddle bands had been a decade earlier.

The duet formula was as simple as it was effective. The guitar player provided basic rhythm chords and usually sang the lower part, the melody line. The mandolin player (traditionally the guitarist's brother) would play whatever little instrumental work there was to do while singing the higher harmony, up in the tenor range. Most of the duets were ballad singers, in either the mountain or sentimental "parlor" tradition, and the best of them produced some of the most hauntingly beautiful vocal work the country people had ever heard.

The Blue Sky Boys were not asked to record until 1936, but they probably couldn't have recorded before then even if they had been asked. They were just kids (sixteen and eighteen years old) from Hickory, North Carolina, when they first stepped up to a Victor microphone. Their family name was Bolick, oddly Eastern European-sounding for mountain people. Bill was the older and played the mandolin, while younger brother Earl played the guitar and sang lead. It's odd, too, that they were pushed into the guitar-mandolin mold. They had always carried a fiddler (usually Homer "Pappy" Sherrill), and Bill was as inclined to play the guitar as the mandolin, but the Monroe Brothers were setting the woods on fire in the Carolinas then—without a fiddler—so Bill and Earl Bolick were asked to drop the fiddle and forced into copying someone they had scarcely heard. The result was totally unlike the Monroe Brothers, and the Blue Sky Boys were the absolute, consummate perfection of the vocal duet.

Mandolinist Bill Bolick says that when he and Earl decided to become a duet, they wanted to be the best. The Delmores had done it right, but the others were sloppy, not caring that both singers were often singing the same part. The Blue Sky Boys developed a blend that was technically superb. They hit each note in perfect harmony, never crossing over and getting the same tone from both their voices. When they performed the old traditional ballad "Mary of the Wild Moor," they sang each word as if it meant something; and when they came to the line " 'Twas on a cold winter's night," the word *night* was rested on and blended with an uncanny dual inflection. The Blue Sky Boys still perform occasionally, and their harmony is still the best ever. Technique aside, their music is moving, sincere, and totally absorbing.

BLUEGRASS

The first Victor Bluebird recordings by the Blue Sky Boys appeared in the Victor catalog in 1936, the same year that Victor made the first recordings of another great duet, the Monroe Brothers from western Kentucky.

Today a handpainted sign on Bill Monroe's battered mandolin case reads "ORIGINAL BLUEGRASS MUSIC SINCE 1927." That's when he and his brothers started playing together. Some date the birth of bluegrass as 1939, when Bill worked up his classic arrangement of the "New Muleskinner Blues," the first song in his characteristic "bluegrass time." Others date it as 1946, when Bill and his Blue Grass Boys recorded "Will You Be Lovin' Another Man?" with Earl Scruggs on the banjo. There are still others, and a lot of them, who date the birth of bluegrass from the 1936 Victor release of "What Would You Give in Exchange for Your Soul?" by Bill and Charlie Monroe.

This popular gospel tune was not in a bluegrass style as we know it today. It was just a duet with some tasteful mandolin backup, but it was a tremendously popular recording in the Carolinas, enhancing the already enviable reputation the Monroes had established on some of the major country radio stations. It seemed almost unbelievable that the Monroes and the Bolicks, using such a similar vocal and instrumental format, could have been so entirely different. The Blue Sky Boys used their guitar and mandolin to enhance what was essentially an old-time mountain ballad singing style. Bill and Charlie Monroe used their instruments and voices in a style that had all the excitement of the old-time fiddle bands at their best—their hell-for-leather instrumentation and the breakneck rapport that existed between Charlie's surging guitar runs and Bill's sprinting mandolin. It laid the real groundwork for the style that was later to be known as bluegrass.

The Monroes could sing the high ranges. They had a quality to their music that later became known as drive, a pounding rhythm unable to contain itself as they raced through songs like "Roll in My Sweet Baby's Arms" and "New River Train." Even their slow numbers had a beat; tunes like "Song of Old Kentucky" and "I Dreamed I Searched Heaven for You" were done in three-quarter time, but they moved along in a way that made listeners feel Bill and Charlie couldn't wait to get the song over with and get on to the next fast one. Charlie's thumb and finger pick walked all over the bass strings, supplying unexpected runs totally unlike the bland rhythm of Earl Bolick and the others, and his voice was rich with a unique western Kentucky warmth that would make him one of the most popular singers in the South for decades.

Bill Monroe was something really different. His tenor voice was good and high, even though it lacked the technical perfection of the Delmores and the Bolicks, and it danced around and over his older brother's full-bodied lead with joyous exuberance. He wasn't content to play the straight melody line as most of the old-time mandolin players did. He brought a real sense of musicianship to his work, playing wild, improvisational mandolin breaks all over the little eight-stringed instrument's short fingerboard. Whatever the negative aspects of the Monroes' personal relationship—problems that would lead to their eventual breakup at the peak of their popularity—they weren't evident in the dynamic and exciting music that had made them a household name in thousands of farmhouses and mountain cabins even before the release of their first Victor records.

The Delmore Brothers, the Monroes, the Bolicks, and the other great duets were the country music rage through the middle of the 1930s, as the recording world was emerging from the Depression and starting to record some of the traditional style music again. Some of the bands coming up then, such as the one headed by old-time fiddler J. E. Mainer, saw the advantages of adding a vocal duet to their groups, giving rise to a tradition that could be called the singing string band, the direct predecessor of the bluegrass band. Instrumentally and vocally, some of these groups were amazingly like the bluegrass bands that followed them a decade later. But there was another band, essentially an old-time string band, that was making a name for itself around Knoxville, Tennessee. It was an old-time sounding group, but its leader was a singing fiddler named Roy Acuff, a transitional figure in bridging a gap that would widen as years passed: the gap between the old-time string fiddle band and the Nashville singing star.

Roy Acuff joined the "Grand Ole Opry" in 1938. His forceful, emotional voice and his zany hillbilly stage act quickly made him the hottest thing in country music, a sort of show-biz reconciliation between the concept of the older bands and the "star" pattern established before his death by singer Jimmie Rodgers. He fiddled and sang; his dobroist, Pete "Brother Oswald" Kirby, blackened his teeth and did raucous banjo duets with "Cousin" Rachel Veach while Acuff played with a yo-yo, balanced his fiddle bow on his nose, and bellowed melancholy versions of "The Wreck on the Highway" and "Wabash Cannonball." He was selling entertainment as well as music, and the audiences loved him for it.

The Roy Acuff concept of show-biz hillbillyism was subtle, but would have far-reaching effects on the future sound and shape of country music.

17

BLUEGRASS

As corny as Oswald's blackened teeth and the bow-balancing act were, they were elevating country music from the world of dancing feet pounding a barn floor, of front-porch fiddlers, of sullen old women singing the old British ballads as they shelled peas. Acuff was a passable fiddler and a great traditional singer, but his product wasn't specifically music. It was country music as entertainment. He was an entertainer who also happened to be a good singer, and it was his personality as well as his music that endeared him to his audience. Roy Acuff's fame spread as the post-Depression years became the war years. Things were moving faster, and country music was growing up.

2

Bill Monroe

THE ALTERNATIVE

The development of country music as a pop style didn't stop with the bombing of Pearl Harbor. Hollywood and Detroit were turning much of their production capacity toward defense, but just as swing seemed to be enjoying its greatest popularity in the war-torn 1940s, so did hillbilly music reach a greater level of acceptance than it had ever known before. Tennessee and Arkansas mountaineers were sharing barracks space with men from Wisconsin and New Jersey, and the cultural exchange sent many southerners home with a taste for Glenn Miller. Not surprisingly, many northern families were somewhat bewildered when their boys came home with a taste for Roy Acuff.

Acuff was one of the most popular stars in the country during those war years. His "Precious Jewel," "Lonely Mound of Clay," and "Wabash Cannonball" were as well known to GIs as were the tunes of the Andrews Sisters.

But it wasn't hillbilly music in the barracks that gave most Americans their first dose of music with a rural flavor. Most Americans had become avid moviegoers during the Depression, and everyone seemed to love those flickering thrillers—the Westerns.

Perhaps it was Jimmie Rodgers' popularity that encouraged the Western stars to pick up a guitar and start singing. Or it may have been that some movie producer felt the new talking films needed something besides thundering hooves and banging six-guns to sustain audience attention.

BLUEGRASS

Whatever the reasons, by the time the war had begun, Texans Gene Autry and Tex Ritter were shooting and singing their way into the ranks of Hollywood's highest-paid stars.

Out in the wartime West, GIs and their dates were dancing to the music of Bob Wills and his Texas Playboys, a southwestern dance orchestra that called its music western swing and was turning out hits like "San Antonio Rose." Western swing was becoming the latest thing in country music, and compared to its brass sections and heavy dance-floor beat, slick Hollywood bands like the Sons of the Pioneers sounded pure hayseed.

The music of the West was a conglomeration of styles. Many of the early settlers in Texas and Oklahoma came from the hills of Tennessee and Kentucky, and their fiddle styles became mixed with songs of the cattle country. The Mexican bands had multiple fiddles and trumpets, and the sounds of blues, jazz, and related styles came in from Louisiana. It was a different tradition and an eclectic one that was being pushed on the country music market.

The crossing of country and western music created a valid hybrid and was certainly instrumental in making "country and western" a more marketable product. People had moved west in search of change. Most were not tied to tradition and actively sought new lives and new ways of doing things. These attitudes were reflected in their music, and these same attitudes were being accepted as the Nashville industry latched on to western music.

In 1940 the "Grand Ole Opry" was quick to hire a western group—Pee Wee King and his Golden West Cowboys. King brought the accordion and electric guitar to the "Opry" stage, and the traditional stars found themselves having to appear in ten-gallon hats and gaudy cowboy garb in order to give the audience what it wanted.

Phony cowboys with drums and electric guitars were becoming the favorites of the "Opry" and "National Barn Dance" stages. Some, like Ernest Tubb, were from the West. Others, like Pee Wee King and Roy Rogers, were not. A lot of money was being made and a lot of misconceptions were being created about the nature of country music. Some of the old-timers resisted the changes and found themselves playing to increasingly localized audiences, farther and farther back in the hills.

Probably the only country star of the era who could afford to keep his sound the same was Roy Acuff, whose reputation had been well enough established during the war. Others had to change, and the identity of country music was changing right along with them. The old styles were dying, and some, like Bill Monroe, knew that something had to be done to bring traditional music up to the new standards of sophistication. There was still life and fire in the old-time music, even if Nashville wasn't interested in pushing it, and Monroe intended to prove it.

Bill Monroe had been a star of the "Opry" when the war broke out. Although they had been doing well as a team, Bill and his brother Charlie had abandoned the old Monroe Brothers act in 1938. Both were extremely strong musical personalities, and the two bigger-than-life egos had found they could no longer work together.

Charlie hired another mandolin player and was soon to develop a distinctive band style of his own. But younger brother Bill was out to prove that he was something more than a famous guitar player's kid brother. He hired a good guitar man, a bass player, and the best fiddle player he could find. They rehearsed solidly for months, and when twenty-nine-year-old Bill Monroe and his group, called the Blue Grass Boys, auditioned for the "Grand Ole Opry" in 1939, they were ready.

The incredibly high-tenor singer and phenomenal mandolin player who was thrilling WSM audiences through the early 1940s had grown up in the western Kentucky village of Rosine, between Louisville and Paducah. It was a musical family, with fiddlers on both sides, and the impression left on young Bill by his Uncle Pen and a local Negro blues guitarist, Arnold Schultz, dominated the musical ideas of the shy, introspective farm boy.

Bill's older brothers, Charlie and Birch, took to music at an early age, with Charlie playing the guitar and Birch the fiddle. The mandolin was left to Bill—the last choice of the last chooser. Stubborn and determined, Bill decided to take the little eight-stringed instrument and show the world that the proud Kentuckian wasn't to be second to anyone.

Charlie and Birch went north to find work, and when their parents died, teen-aged Bill left home to follow his brothers to the oil refineries around Chicago. They played in their spare time, but when the WLS "Barn Dance" formed a touring company of square dancers, the three brothers saw a chance to escape the refineries and get into show business. Birch left the act, and Charlie and Bill's fortunes led them to several stations throughout the Midwest. They were seasoned veterans by 1934, when they found themselves becoming one of the most popular acts working out of Columbia, South Carolina.

The Monroe Brothers were a tremendous hit in the Carolinas by 1936, when Victor approached them with a recording contract. Two gospel numbers were cut that rapidly became some of the biggest sellers the South had seen. Radios across the Carolinas were tuning in the Monroe Brothers, from Charlotte, Columbia, Greenville, and Raleigh, but it seemed the more the brothers worked together, the less they could get along. They were at the top of the field in 1938, after their move to Raleigh, but could no longer go it as a duet.

It may have been in the back of Bill's mind to outdo Charlie. He had sounds in his head that echoed from his childhood and his travels, and he knew that if he worked hard enough, these sounds would take him places. But he couldn't do it with just another duet. A bass was needed to add extra depth and rhythm, and a good fiddler was essential if he was to put into action the ideas he had carried since his boyhood days of the square dances and his Uncle Pen, whose memory Bill almost worshipped.

It was the fall of 1939, and George Dewey Hay, the "Solemn Old Judge" of WSM, had found Bill's new band worthy of inclusion in the cast of the "Grand Ole Opry." Bill could scarcely wait to show what he could do, and audiences all over the huge WSM listening radius sensed that there seldom had been anything like the new Blue Grass Boys on the "Opry" stage. It was just a four-piece string band, but it had a beat that was actually part of the music itself, not an extraneous addition like the drums of Bob Wills and Pee Wee King. It was traditional music, played on the traditional instruments, but there was a surging drive to it, a power and explosiveness that had never been heard within the limits of the old-time music. Bill was singing high, soaring blues and was establishing as his trademark an old Jimmie Rodgers tune that Bill called the "Muleskinner Blues." His powerful, intense tenor and the driving blues fiddling of Art Wooten gave the old Rodgers tune a new sound that almost took the roof off the "Opry" house every time he sang it. They were doing complicated gospel quartets and fiddle breakdowns better than anyone had done them before, and not too much time passed before the Blue Grass Boys were one of the most popular touring bands to work out of the WSM studios.

Victor recorded this new band just before the war, and these recordings gave Bill's music an even wider audience. He was making changes in his sound, and by the time the Blue Grass Boys were recorded for the first time, he had hired a mellow-voiced Carolinian named Clyde Moody to play guitar and sing lead, a comic bass player named "Cousin" Wilbur West-brook, and a fantastic fiddler named Tommy Magness. The thrust and urgency of this group was successfully captured on wax, and many of the performances were masterpieces.

Bill Monroe often said over the years that the first song he ever performed in a style consciously conceived as his own was "Muleskinner Blues." His performance was considerably faster than the old Jimmie Rodgers version, and he added a characteristic beat that has come to be known as bluegrass time. Bill played guitar on that original cut, and he may have gotten the ideas from the black guitarist he had heard as a boy back in Rosine, or from Jimmie Rodgers, or even from his brother Charlie. But regardless of where the ideas came from, this rendition of "Muleskinner Blues" had a swooping, pounding beat to it that gave the tune an incredible forward thrust. Bill's singing was very much in the bluegrass category on that number, and Tommy Magness' hair-raising blues fiddle dove in and around Bill's voice in a way that made that 1940 Victor cut one of the most exciting performances in country music history.

Much of Monroe's prewar Victor output was similar to what other groups were doing in country music. Bill and Clyde Moody sang a standard duet tune, "I Wonder If You Feel the Way I Do," and others of that type, but tunes like "Muleskinner" really set his music apart. Tommy Magness played a version of the old fiddle tune "Katy Hill" that was faster than anything most fiddle players would even attempt, and Bill was making some of the first recordings in country music of solo mandolin—the fiddlelike "Tennessee Blues" and a jazzy blues thing called "Honky Tonk Swing," which showed one of his first attempts to modernize within the framework of tradition. Bill and Wilbur Westbrook sang a duet, a lonesome tune called "In the Pines," and the haunting, mournful sound of this performance had the chill of the mountains in it, a soulful, emotional sound that was the distilled essence of mountain music and mountain life. It was an early example of the "high, lonesome sound," a phrase that would come to characterize the music of Bill Monroe.

Bill was probably the most creative musician at WSM during the early war years. He had a sound in his head that would not let him rest until he had found the right musicians to give it expression. He had become well enough established at the "Opry" by the early 1940s to feel safe in experimenting with new sounds and new musicians. He was using some of the best fiddlers of the day in his band, and by 1942 he had hired his first banjo player. Dave Akeman was tall and lean, and he could make audiences laugh under his famous stage name, Stringbean.

BLUEGRASS

WSM and the "Grand Ole Opry" were providing the Blue Grass Boys with thousands of fans, and Bill Monroe was among the top stars of the day. Brother Charlie Monroe and his Kentucky Pardners were still popular down in the Carolinas—as popular as Bill in many areas—and the younger Monroe seemed to resent the fact that his brother was doing well as a Victor recording artist. Charlie was an impressive man and an outstanding performer, and his formidable shadow caused Bill to switch from Victor to Columbia Records. Bill and the Boys cut several sides for Columbia in the mid-1940s, and these numbers provided Bill with some enormous national hits—"Footprints in the Snow," "Blue Moon of Kentucky," and "Kentucky Waltz."

Bill's show was on the road continually, and he could fill his huge circus tent sometimes two and three times at one location, bringing in thousands of dollars in revenue every night of the week. But despite his immense popularity in person and on records Bill Monroe seemed dissatisfied with himself and his sound. Stringbean was a good banjo player, but his old-time style was unsuited to the new, smooth sound of the band. Then, much to the bluegrass historian's dismay, there was the Pee Wee King influence in the person of Sally (Mrs. Howard) Forrester and her accordion. Bill was trying to bring the fiddle sounds of his Kentucky boyhood, the vocal sound of the Monroe Brothers, and the blues sound all into the totality of a full band sound, and it was a struggle.

By the time Bill recorded his best-selling Columbia material, he had already hired a pudgy young swing fiddler from Florida named Chubby Wise and an excellent lead singer from the mountains of eastern Tennessee named Lester Flatt.

Lester was a fine traditional singer, and a recent stint as a tenor with Charlie Monroe had served to put his voice up in the ranges where Bill was used to singing. They made one of the finest duets ever heard.

Flatt had been with Monroe for about a year when Bill auditioned a young banjo player from North Carolina. His name was Earl Scruggs, and his style of three-finger banjo playing was something almost entirely new to most country music fans. Earl had perfected the three-finger "roll" that had been used in his native Cleveland County for years, a style that was used by the great Snuffy Jenkins and others. Earl was still in his teens when he smoothed out the sound so that he could take a flowing, driving banjo solo on almost any kind of number—something that had never been done before.

24

Bill still had his doubts as to the limitations of the style, but Earl Scruggs was given a job with the Blue Grass Boys that day in 1945. Bill Monroe's decision to give a young boy from North Carolina a job proved to be one of the most important moves of his career.

The Blue Grass Boys had been popular from the beginning at WSM, but it was the band that included Lester Flatt, Earl Scruggs, and Chubby Wise that really caught fire. Audiences just couldn't believe that anyone could play the banjo like Earl Scruggs. It was so fast and smooth, and there were so many notes, but all the melody and everything else was right there in the shower of banjo music. The crowds would roar every time Earl stepped to the microphone.

Lester Flatt's outstanding, beautifully inflected lead voice blended with Bill's on the duets, trios, and quartets as none of Monroe's lead singers had done before, and his rhythm guitar playing, with its characteristic bass runs, gave the band a unity of sound that was as unique as it was excellent.

Bill was using his close-chorded mandolin for an almost drumlike rhythm effect, giving the band a heavy, syncopated timing that was the extension of the old square-dance beat put into use as the entire rhythmic structure of a band style. His singing was as high and strong as ever, and his solo mandolin work was rapidly bringing the instrument out of the forgotten corners of country music and into a position of esteem it had never before enjoyed.

The bass was always featured in Monroe's bands, and he often used his brother Birch as the band's bassist. He also used the talents of an outstanding musician named Howard Watts (known as Cedric Rainwater, a comic personna) on the upright bass.

Over the top of the banjo, bass, guitar, and mandolin, and riding over the vocal solos, duets, trios, and quartets, flowed the fiddle of Chubby Wise, some of the loveliest fiddle every played. Chubby combined the almost classical tone and sweetness of swing fiddle with the blues sound upon which Bill insisted, adding his own subtle soulfulness that stamped its profound influence on the bluegrass fiddle style.

This whole band, in fact, marked the final maturity of an entirely new music style, traditional yet somehow vitally modern, that was to develop within a few short years into a whole new movement in American music.

It is doubtful whether any other band in the history of country music had the effect on the country people that the Blue Grass Boys did in those years just after the war. Bill's "Wal-rite Paint" radio show was never missed, nor were his weekly appearances on the "Grand Ole Opry." His traveling road show (and accompanying exhibition baseball teams) was breaking records everywhere it played, even in the most remote mountain areas. People were clamoring to see this band in action, and they were never disappointed.

Those years saw hundreds of young mountain banjo pickers giving up the old styles and putting on metal finger picks in an attempt to play like Earl Scruggs. The Blue Grass Boys' songs were learned by heart, and new bands coming up (as well as some of the older ones) were deciding that Bill Monroe's great new sound was one to be imitated. Groups all over the South were hunting for banjo pickers who had taken up the "Scruggs style" and had become proficient enough to play it professionally.

The people of the mountains had taken Monroe's music as their own—as the logical evolutionary development of the music they had heard all their lives, jazzed up and speeded up in a way that made it new and alive. But their love of the new Monroe style could not stop the meshing of popular hillbilly styles and popular western music. The world was shrinking, and the lure of the extremes of modernization was too irresistible. The money powers that had been establishing themselves in Nashville were working overtime trying to wrench themselves away from the stigma of rurality.

As the 1950s approached, the darlings of Nashville became those with the least amount of "country" in their voices. Eddy Arnold and George Morgan were favorites, and the songs began leaning away from the time-honored themes of life with the earth and the elements, as more lyrics were being written about smokey honky-tonks and sordid back-alley love affairs.

Bill Monroe's genius was committed to the ideal of moving country music ahead in its *own* direction, not away from the sources of the country experience. But modern Nashville just didn't want to be identified with anything the public might laugh at, or worse, wouldn't spend their money on. Modernization was becoming a cause in itself, and those who didn't mind having their music emasculated and robbed of its inherent greatness followed the banner of the new Nashville.

The powerful web of the Nashville industry was widening. The old live radio broadcasts were almost a thing of the past when the soldiers went off to fight a new war in Korea, and the radio had ceased to be the means of preservation for all the lesser-known bands whose success had once depended upon it. Records were the thing, and most of what Nashville was pressing into 78 rpm wax was intended to be the kind of innocuous pap that would sell to the largest possible market. The big money was just not being put behind the traditional acts.

Records and radio were combining into a new movement in entertainment as the disc jockey became the important new man in the business. The disc jockeys were playing the records that were getting the biggest promotional push from the big labels and talent agencies, and this push was being used to propel only the most commercial acts in the Nashville stable. The great artists in the traditional style were left to go begging.

When Columbia and other labels had begun marketing the music of people like "Fiddlin'" John Carson and Eck Robertson back in the early 1920s, the country people had bought it because it was their music. They could identify with it and appreciate it. Now their music was drifting away from them, or at least drifting away from what it had been. Radio and that new invention the television were becoming as influential in swaying the tastes of the country people as the mail order catalog had been almost a century earlier. They were being told from all sides that the country way was bad, that everyone should want a life like that enjoyed by "Ozzie and Harriet," with two cars and a sprawling house in the suburbs. These were the American goals, and only ignorant yokels were satisfied to live back in the sticks and eat cornbread.

The move was away from the country and country life, as more and more left the hills and farms to find jobs in the North and West. But still, in the deepest mountains, there was an obstinate strain, a refusal to accept change so easily. The mountain people knew what kind of music was their own and what kind wasn't. The sounds and traditions of the banjo and fiddle were deeply woven into the fabric of their lives. It was not so easily removed. Nashville was playing less and less of "their" music, but there was still one star at the "Opry" who was playing it, and playing it better than anyone had before. The man was Bill Monroe, and his fierce pride in his tradition-laden music and country birthright elevated him to an almost godlike status among the people of the rural South.

Bill Monroe and his Blue Grass Boys were still one of the most popular bands throughout Appalachia as the 1940s were left behind, and Monroe's refusal to change—to sell out his heritage for the sake of capital gain—made him a cause for many, something for them to cling to and believe in. Many people in the country felt Bill Monroe was playing the only real country music.

Nashville and the old styles of country music split from one another around 1950. Most followed the Nashville trend, but others followed the Bill Monroe school as the logical advancement of old-time music. Bands playing in the Bill Monroe style started springing up all over the mountain areas, the areas that had been Monroe's most loyal ground. First there were the Stanley Brothers from Virginia, whose records were making them almost as well known as Monroe himself. Then Flatt and Scruggs left Monroe to start their own band. And others who played with Bill in the early days went on to stardom playing the Bill Monroe style themselves: Don Reno, Mac Wiseman, Jim Eanes, Jimmy Martin, Carter Stanley, Sonny Osborne.

The popularity and musical validity of Bill Monroe's old-new style could not be denied, but it could do nothing to stop the bland hybrid that was becoming known as "country and western." The strident electric twang of the new sound was something apart from the pure, nonelectric, totally rural sound of Bill Monroe and his followers.

It was in the early 1950s that people started referring to the Bill Monroe style as "bluegrass."

3

The Stanley Brothers

MOUNTAIN STYLE

The Appalachians are a vast, sweeping range, cutting diagonally down the breadth of the United States. The heart of these mountains is an area that can be found by sticking a tack where the map marks the historic Cumberland Gap and drawing a circle with a radius of about eighty miles. This circle would take you north above Beckley, West Virginia; east to Roanoke, Virginia; south to the western counties of North Carolina; west through the Great Smokies of eastern Tennessee; and north again through the most mountainous areas of eastern Kentucky. Blue grass, the botanical variety, grows far to the west. Bluegrass, the music style, found its principal breeding ground within this imaginary circle deep within the southern mountains.

In the center of this circle, where the long southwestern tip of Virginia wedges its way between the Kentucky and Tennessee borders, lies Dickenson County, Virginia. It lies in the high ridge country, abundant in coal, where little farming is done because the mountainsides are too steep and the valley floors too narrow for plowing or planting. It's a place rich in physical beauty, but it's a hard place to make a living.

There has been little money to be made in Dickenson County since the lumber mills closed down for lack of timber sometime after the Depression. The coal mines are prominent now, but mechanization has made even them an unsteady means of employment. Through the years, increasing numbers of the descendants of the original settlers have moved out of Dickenson County, going to places like Detroit and Flint, Michigan, to find better lives in the havens of northern industry.

They left the mountains around such places as Haysi, Vansant, Clinchco, Fremont, and McClure. McClure isn't on most maps of Virginia. Fremont is, and it's not much more than a little mountain train station. It was in this remote area that a logger named Fitzhugh Stanley married Lucy Smith. He was a widower with six children. She was a widow with one child and was a fine performer on the old-time clawhammer banjo. In the summer of 1925 the Stanleys had a son, whom they named Carter. Two years later, in the winter of 1927, another boy was born, and he was named Ralph.

The two Stanley boys were hardly more than babies when their parents moved to the old Smith homeplace near McClure. It was a little Clinch Mountain farm on an extremely high ridge, a breath-takingly beautiful place with a panoramic view of ridge after hazy ridge, over into Kentucky and down into Tennessee. The beauty of the place made a lasting impression on the two young boys. The images of deep, rolling hills, mountain laurel, lonesome cabins, and aging parents at the old home would appear in the music of the Stanley brothers for many years to come.

Aunts and uncles proliferated on both sides of the family, and all either sang the old mountain ballads or played the old clawhammer five-string. Everyone went to the McClure Baptist Church, where they sang the old "lined-out" hymns—the preacher would sing the lead line and the congregation would sing the "repeats." The tunes of the Baptist hymns were mixed with the melodies of the ballads sung at home, as the sounds of the mountains were being imbedded in the minds of Ralph and Carter Stanley.

There was music around the Stanley household, and much of it flew magically through the air, coming from as far away as central Tennessee and North Carolina. The radio broadcasts from Raleigh and Asheville and the "Opry" were tuned in with regularity, as the Monroe Brothers and Mainer's Mountaineers put thoughts of show business careers into the Stanley brothers' childhood dreams. Carter wasn't even into his teens when he got his first guitar from the mail order catalog. Ralph was soon learning to play his mother's banjo, and the boys began working out duet harmonies together.

The early 1940s saw a lot of young men from Virginia sent off to war. It was early in 1946 before a homesick Carter Stanley came back to the mountain farm from the air force. When Ralph came wandering home from the army later that same year, he found that his older brother had lost no time finding musical employment. The band was called Roy Sykes and the Blue Ridge Mountain Boys, and before long, young Ralph was playing with them too.

The Stanley brothers soon realized they would have to try playing on their own. They left Sykes and took the group's mandolin player, Pee Wee Lambert, with them. They hired a fiddle player and called themselves the Stanley Brothers and the Clinch Mountain Boys and were soon playing on the radio over at Norton, Virginia.

Shortly afterwards they heard of a new show starting up at WCYB in Bristol, Tennessee. It was the famous "Farm and Fun Time," a show that was to feature almost all of the great early bluegrass acts, and it would be the Stanleys' radio home for almost twelve years. WCYB broadcast all over the mountains within that bluegrass circle, and the brothers soon were playing to packed houses throughout the region.

They were playing a cross between the archaic mountain styles and the yet unnamed Bill Monroe style, and it seemed to be just what the mountain people wanted to hear. They performed at the little schoolhouses and theaters and featured a song that was catching on—a tune called "Little Glass of Wine." The song was so well received in 1947 that they were contacted by the Rich-R-Tone Record Company in Johnson City, Tennessee. It was a small label, but many who had recorded for it had gone on to bigger and better things.

The recordings done by the Stanleys for Rich-R-Tone are classic examples of how the old-time music was evolving into bluegrass. Ralph, just twenty at the time, was playing three different styles of banjo: the old clawhammer style, a two-finger style that was being used by popular mountain artist Wade Mainer, and a rudimentary three-finger style that he was probably picking up from the radio work of Earl Scruggs. He and Carter were singing some of the oldest songs of the mountains—songs like "Man of Constant Sorrow"—together with some of the newest Bill Monroe tunes—"Are You Waiting Just for Me?" and "Molly and Tenbrooks." The early Rich-R-Tone sessions were illustrative of the impact and evolutionary effect Monroe's music had on the native Appalachian musicians. The Stanley Brothers' work clearly showed three stages of old-time music as they existed in the mid-1940s: ancient ballads, Mainer-style commercial string band music, and bluegrass.

Ralph and Carter were pretty much in the old-time camp when they went into the studio to record for the first time. It may be safely said that their experimentation with the Monroe sound was due largely to the influence of their mandolin player, Darrell "Pee Wee" Lambert. Lambert, a West Virginian, was a prime example of the effect the dynamic personality of Bill Monroe had on many of the outstanding, creative mountain musicians. Like thousands after him, Lambert was completely taken by Monroe and his music. Monroe's depth and inner drive, his mystique and phenomenal musicianship, reached Lambert in the same way many others were reached, and in many it became almost an obsession. The intensity of Bill Monroe and his music had moved Lambert, and the enthusiasm carried over to the Stanleys. They were soon doing much of Monroe's material, and they were doing it well.

Through the late 1940s, Lambert did most of the tenor singing. A band style was developing, after the Monroe fashion, where the mandolin player also sang tenor. The Stanleys were following that pattern. Pee Wee's voice was as high as Bill's, just as his mandolin playing rivaled that of Monroe in its soulfulness and brilliance. Ralph was perfecting the Scruggs style of playing the banjo, and he sang some of the tenor, though his voice hadn't quite matured into that distinctively eerie mountain tenor that was to become his trademark. Carter was becoming good and solid on the rhythm guitar, and he was quickly turning into a bluegrass lead singer.

Things were going better and better for the brothers. They moved to WPTF in Raleigh and were carrying a full five-piece band, complete with bass and fiddle, when they were approached by Columbia Records' Art Satherly. They had been together only two years and were being asked to record on one of the country's major labels—and on top of everything, it was the same label that Monroe was on. This was a tremendous break for them, and the signing of the Stanley sound to the Columbia label resulted in one of the most artistically successful marriages in the history of bluegrass.

Ralph and Carter and their band had grown immeasurably since the first Rich-R-Tone sides two years earlier. The Columbia material reflected a conscious attempt at working toward a sound distinct from Monroe's but at the same time closer to the one that was establishing itself as "bluegrass." They had left the archaic material behind, but they were no longer trying to record copies of Monroe's work. The Stanleys had a softer sound, but with more of the lonesome quality of the mountains in it—sounds taken from the old church singing and the lonesomeness of the mountains themselves.

Much of the lonesome sound in Monroe's work came from the inclusion of blues, more or less from the black traditions.

The emotional quality of the Stanley Brothers' voices has never been equaled. It was not forced or theatrical. It was reserved and subtle but unmistakable and incredibly moving. They were trying to establish themselves as a duet, and their voices blended splendidly in tunes like "It's Never Too Late" and "Too Late to Cry." Probably the most memorable tunes from the Columbia sessions were the trios with Lambert—some of the most hauntingly eerie performances ever recorded. Carter wrote most of them and sang them in his distinctively moving way, joined by Ralph on the tenor, with Lambert adding an even higher part: "A Vision of Mother," "Drunkard's Hell," and the classics "White Dove," "The Fields Have Turned Brown," and "The Angels Are Singing." The greatest of these was the chillingly mournful "Lonesome River."

Only a few of the Columbia cuts tried openly to emulate the Monroe sound: "Let Me Be Your Friend" and "The Old Home." The latter was a number very much along the lines of the Monroe-Flatt-Scruggs tune "I'm Going Back to Old Kentucky." There is evidence that Monroe considered the inclusion of the mandolin and Scruggs-style banjo an attempt at cashing in on his sound. He wasn't flattered, and by 1950 he had left Columbia, feeling that the Stanleys were too much like the Blue Grass Boys.

There is evidence also that Ralph wasn't sold on the idea of being a full-time musician. He had wanted to become a veterinarian after leaving the army, but Carter had talked him into playing the banjo for a living. By 1951 Ralph decided to leave the Clinch Mountain Boys, at least for a short period. Carter moved to Nashville and became Bill Monroe's guitar player.

Carter spent an historic half year with the Blue Grass Boys. He had developed into one of the outstanding lead singers of his time, and Monroe knew he had to get the band into the recording studio while Stanley was with him. Bill had signed with Decca in 1950 and proceeded to record a string of classics, notably a recut of his "Muleskinner Blues" and the legendary "Uncle Pen." His songs with Carter were no less classic. "Cabin of Love" and "Sugar Coated Love" were two duets, and there were also some great gospel quartets, the best of which was probably the imploring and ghostly "Get Down on Your Knees and Pray." Ralph was injured in an auto accident during this period, and when he recovered, the brothers reunited and moved back to WCYB and the "Farm and Fun Time."

The Stanleys used two mandolinists of note during this period: Curly Sechler (long-time veteran of the Flatt and Scruggs band) and Bobby Osborne. Osborne was drafted into the army in 1952, and the Stanleys' recording output was slow until 1954, when they signed a contract with Mercury Records.

Mercury had signed Flatt and Scruggs almost immediately after they left Monroe's band in 1948. Lester and Earl evidently saw a better opportunity over at Columbia and signed there in 1950. Every label had its bluegrass band then, and possibly the Stanleys were signed by Mercury to fill the gap left by the exit of Flatt and Scruggs.

The Clinch Mountain Boys' sound seemed to alter slightly with each label-jump they made. The Rich-R-Tone sound was old-time, the Columbia sound rich and lonesome. When Carter, Ralph, Jimmy Williams, Art Stamper, and George Shuffler walked into the Owen Bradley studios in Nashville that August day in 1953, they made what has been considered some of the most exciting, hard-driving bluegrass music ever played.

To say that the first Mercury session was hot would be a woeful understatement. Carter's lead singing was strong and self-assured, and Ralph was sending his hard, mountain tenor right up through the rafters. The younger Stanley was playing his banjo hard and loud, establishing once and for all the Stanley-style of bluegrass banjo. Williams played some inspired Monroe-style mandolin, and Stamper played breaks and fiddle backup that are still talked about. Giving the session an almost unbelievable forward thrust was bassist Shuffler, playing some of the most complicated bluegrass bass ever heard. Only four numbers were recorded: "(Say) Won't You Be Mine?" "The Weary Heart You Stole Away," "I'm Lonesome Without You," and "Our Last Goodbye." All became standards against which the group would be measured.

Not all of their Mercury sessions were as tight as the first, but much of what they did ranks with the very best bluegrass ever recorded. Several cuts were gospel quartets, great numbers like "Calling from Heaven," "Let Me Walk, Lord, by Your Side," and "Cry from the Cross," while their secular songs reflected the synthesis of their lonesome Columbia material and the tight drive they had been developing since leaving Columbia—"Loving You Too Well," "Who'll Call You Sweetheart?" and "Lonesome and Blue."

The Stanleys' work for Mercury, like that done by Flatt and Scruggs' stay for the same label, was one of the high-water marks of early bluegrass. They had some great sidemen with them—fiddlers Benny Martin, Howdy

Forrester, Ralph Mayo, Chubby Anthony, and Joe Meadows and their high-grade mandolinists, Jimmy Williams, Pee Wee Lambert, Bill Lowe, and George Shuffler—and their duet singing was extremely powerful. But there were cold winds blowing on the entire field of traditional country music; a Memphis label called Sun Records was producing hits by rhythm and blues-oriented country boys named Presley, Cash, and Perkins. The whole complexion of popular music shifted toward rock 'n' roll, and the big sound in country music became "rockabilly." The Stanley Brothers were pressured into attempting contrived boogie-woogie tunes that were totally unsuited to their style, numbers like "So Blue" and a version of "Blue Moon of Kentucky" that resembled the Elvis Presley version more than the original Bill Monroe classic. One of their last numbers for Mercury was a trite country "weeper" called "If That's the Way You Feel," which featured (much to the chagrin of their fans) a whiny, electric pedal steel guitar. The Stanleys weren't playing their own music anymore, and Mercury was dissatisfied with their work and the general sales of country music. By 1958 the Stanley Brothers had left Mercury Records and gone to work in Florida.

The ax had fallen for all but the biggest of the older country artists, and bluegrass—the most traditional and least commercial of all country music styles—nearly perished. Some of the traditional country and bluegrass acts found refuge at the "Suwannee River Jamboree" television program in Florida, and the next several years saw the Stanley Brothers and the Clinch Mountain Boys working out of Live Oak, Florida. They toured the deep South under the auspices of the Jim Walter Corporation, makers of prefab homes.

The late 1950s saw another phenomenon in the music world that was probably as good for bluegrass as the rock 'n' roll movement was destructive to country music. The Kingston Trio and the Tarriers had major hits before 1960 that marked the culmination of a movement in folk music that had existed in many urban and college centers since the late 1940s. The trend was toward tradition, and the folk music sound became the latest addition to the popular music market.

Nashville was groping for a way to contend with the new southern rock sensations like Jerry Lee Lewis and Carl Perkins. It worked overtime to squelch the real country elements that were becoming more of an embarrassment with each new "rockabilly" hit. At least one Nashville label, Starday, saw the folk craze as a limited way out. Starday began recording old-time artists and bluegrass bands right and left, and a seemingly endless array of Starday LPs stamped clearly "with five-string banjo" flooded the market.

Starday's Don Pierce was groping, too. He made the mistake of not familiarizing himself with the market, and many of his releases had the kind of gaudy Nashville packaging job that the sophisticated urban folk audiences loathed. Pierce was also guilty of some questionable marketing techniques, such as releasing the same song two and three times under different titles. The Starday records seemed to come out one after the other, sometimes several at a crush. If the cut wasn't an immediate seller, it would be taken out of the catalog. Pierce's venture was not a totally successful one, but he did record some exceptionally good bluegrass (as well as some very mediocre bluegrass), and one of his principal groups was the Stanley Brothers.

Much of the Stanley Brothers' Starday material was recorded in Florida, and most of it was superb. Not much attention has been given to the Starday work. It's generally overshadowed either by the fabulous Mercury cuts or by later work, but the short-lived Starday period was one of the most artistically rewarding periods of their career. A great deal of the Starday work has become part of the standard bluegrass repertoire, magnificent performances of tunes like "Ridin' the Midnight Train," "Carolina Mountain Home," "Just a Little at a Time," "Gonna Paint the Town," and the classic among classics, "Rank Stranger." Their band during this period included some of the finest sidemen: fiddlers Ralph Mayo and Chubby Anthony and mandolinists Bill Napier and Curly Lambert.

The folk market was just opening up for the Stanley Brothers when they moved from Starday to King, a Cincinnati-based label. The "Swanee River" show eventually folded, but they were still using Live Oak as a home base, which necessitated a tremendous amount of travel and subsequent strain, especially since their appearances at the many college folk festivals around the country had increased their tour mileage.

The first King LP probably supplied as many songs to the basic bluegrass song bag as any ever issued—"How Mountain Girls Can Love," "Think of What You've Done," and Ralph's classic instrumental, "Clinch Mountain Backstep." Their band in the early King days was one of the best, including fiddler Ralph Mayo, mandolinist Bill Napier, and bassist Al "Towzer Murphy" Elliot (Carter may be heard calling their names on the spoken exchange portion of their great version of the old mountain tune "Train 45").

THE STANLEY BROTHERS

The folk music crowd was really latching on to the bluegrass sound during the early 1960s, and the more traditional a band's sound, the better they liked it. The Stanley Brothers—the most traditional of all the name bluegrass bands—were the darlings of the folk-traditionalists. They were no strangers to the college folk festival or sophisticated urban coffeehouse, and their travels were taking them almost everywhere in the country. King was releasing album after album as the Stanley name became known all over the world.

But like Don Pierce of Starday in the late 1950s, Syd Nathan of King Records didn't seem to know exactly who the Stanley Brothers' audience was. Older Stanley fans as well as the new ones wanted the old bluegrass sound, with lots of good mountain fiddle and mandolin, but Nathan wouldn't go along with it. He encouraged them to drop the fiddle and mandolin and use only the banjo and lead guitar. Ralph Mayo found himself with less and less to do at the recording sessions, and Napier found himself playing lead guitar.

The guitar hadn't been widely used as a lead instrument in bluegrass. It has a mellow sound, and its chorded, open-string rhythm has always been essential in providing a backup for the other instruments. But the usual requirements for lead playing bluegrass were a brittle, staccato sound, like the ring of the banjo and the sharp crispness of the mandolin. Flatt and Scruggs had used lead guitar sparingly, and Bill Monroe used it only twice or three times, but the guitar was becoming the primary lead instrument in the Stanley band, and traditionalists winced with each new King release.

Guitarists Bill Napier and George Shuffler did some excellent work on the Stanley records, but Ralph seemed to be getting fewer chances to play his banjo. King was seemingly trying to cash in on the success they had had with the Delmore Brothers' postwar recordings. The Delmores had used guitar and harmonica, and it wasn't hard to foresee the intrusion of the totally nonbluegrass sound of the mouth harp on the Stanleys' records.

Ralph and Carter were busier than ever, but there were signs that the strain was becoming too great, both physically and emotionally. There is evidence that alcohol was becoming a problem in the group, and it was taking its toll on the band's creative half and front man, Carter Stanley. By the middle of the 1960s, Carter was clearly not a well man. It was a sad thing to see the Stanley Brothers toward the end of Carter's life, and saddest for those who loved their music the most.

Life on the road was hard. They would be home only once or twice a month, and a bluegrass band in those days—even the best of the bands —would drive all night and half the next day for a few hundred dollars. Hard drinking was common; it was a life of boredom, and alcohol helped lift the spirits that so often had reason to be low. The pay was low and the work was hard, and toward the last the Stanleys seldom carried sidemen—it was cheaper to pick up musicians at each location, and, after all, the Stanley sound had enough adherents among bluegrass musicians that it wasn't hard to find one or two who would fit. But the music suffered, and often Carter would be so ill he was unable to contribute much to the show. But he had to go on.

The Stanley Brothers toured northern Europe, a fateful mistake in view of Carter's failing health. They took a band with them, but after their return to the States their road band often included only one other man, guitarist George Shuffler. Sometimes Carter felt well enough to sing, but other times he didn't. By the fall of 1966 it had become clear that Carter was no longer able to continue.

They played at the WWVA "Jamboree" one Saturday night in October, and the following day did a show at Bill Monroe's park in Bean Blossom, Indiana. Carter's voice was little more than a shadow of what it had been only a few years before, but he sang with the strength of conviction and depth of feeling that characterized everything he had ever done. It was the last show he was ever to play. Two months later he was dead.

The passing of Carter Stanley marked the first death of a major figure in the field of bluegrass music. He had traveled thousands of miles for two decades, creating some glorious bluegrass music. This man, only forty-one at his death, had made tremendous contributions to a style that has become today a major movement in the world of music. He was buried at McClure, in the old Smith family graveyard. The grave is on the highest piece of ground on the little mountain farm, overlooking thousands of acres of forested ridges. The mountains about which Carter Stanley never tired of writing and singing, and from which he had traveled so far, stretched for miles below the high Virginia mountaintop. Bill Monroe sang at the graveside services. Carter Stanley had come home to stay.

Carter had always been the dominant figure, the older brother. He had written most of the songs, he had done the talking on stage. He had selected and arranged material. He had done almost all the singing. Ralph generally had come off as an instrumentalist and harmony singer who did some of the business chores. Now it was the quiet brother, the one who always was content to surrender the limelight to the older man, who had to make the important decision. Ralph was still in his thirties, young enough to take up another line of work. What was he going to do?

Stanley Brothers fans are probably more emotionally involved with their music than anyone in bluegrass. The Stanleys' music has twice the elusive quality of mountain soul as anyone else's. It lacks the technical wizardry of some other bands, but it hits its listeners at the gut level and takes hold with a grip that refuses to let go. Ralph Stanley's fans made his decision for him. A memorial concert was held for Carter Stanley near Washington D.C., in the spring of 1967. Ralph Stanley was there with his new version of the Clinch Mountain Boys.

Between 1946 and 1966 the Stanley Brothers had succeeded in creating a style within a style. Theirs was a totally mountain-sounding form of bluegrass, and their influence was such that scores of outstanding musicians grew up listening to their music. *Stanley-style band, Stanley-type singer,* and *Ralph Stanley-style banjo picker* had become common terms in the field of bluegrass. Hundreds of youngsters were working to emulate the sounds of Ralph and Carter, and one of these was a nineteen-year-old from Lebanon, Ohio; named Larry Sparks.

Larry Sparks had a great deal going for him when he stepped into the very large shoes of Carter Stanley in the early days of 1967. His voice was deep and mature, highly reminiscent of the late King-period Carter. He had a great stage presence, and his rhythm and lead guitar playing matched or surpassed anything heard in the Stanley bands of the past. The Clinch Mountain Boys of 1968 included Stanley, Sparks, guitarist Melvin Goins, and fiddler Curly Ray Cline (both veterans of the old Lonesome Pine Fiddlers), and their appearance at the bluegrass festivals not only displayed a vitality that had long since been missing from the Stanley Brothers act but also showed the bluegrass world that the Stanley sound was completely intact.

Sparks stayed with Ralph long enough to get the Clinch Mountain Boys back on their feet. He was a powerful performer and had become a star among the younger generation of bluegrass traditionalists. He felt he was capable of leading his own group. He left Ralph to form his own successful band, the Lonesome Ramblers. But the Stanley sound had so many imitators that Ralph could have his pick of any number of capable musicians. His choice was a young Kentuckian named Roy Lee Centers.

The addition of Centers produced a band that was probably the finest traditional-style bluegrass band ever to be formed since the Golden Age of the 1950s. Centers' voice bore an uncanny likeness to Carter's in his best days—the Mercury years. The group was further enhanced by the addition of two sixteen-year-olds from eastern Kentucky: guitarist Keith Whitley and mandolinist Rick Skaggs. Ralph had found them playing at one of his personal appearances and was moved that these two teen-agers had chosen the Stanley sound as their means of musical expression.

Ralph probably never had a better band than the one in the early 1970s. With Keith Whitley and Rick Skaggs in the band, he knew he could retire when he felt like it and still leave someone to carry on his sound. But Whitley and Skaggs left to play with other bands, and Ralph maintained a high standard of music in the group. He had experienced a hard life on the road, a life with trouble and tragedy. But he could hardly have been prepared for the tragedy that befell him in the spring of 1974.

Roy Lee Centers, the twenty-nine-year-old singer who was probably the best of the Stanley-style lead singers, was murdered near his home in Jackson, Kentucky. He was the third young bluegrass musician to die within a very short period of time (In 1973 Clarence White had been killed in an auto accident and Neal Allen, Red Allen's son, had died of pneumonia.). The fact that his death was an unbelievably violent one sent the bluegrass world into a state of shock.

Death had again left Ralph Stanley mourning not only a friend but someone upon whose talents he had depended. He had spoken of retirement, and the world of bluegrass wondered if this might not be the final blow. He had been doing so well; he had a great band, and the festivals had made his life as a professional musician much easier than it had ever been. Now he would have to start over or quit. Again, bluegrass held its breath.

Ralph's own festival, the annual Carter Stanley Memorial Festival, was coming up. Everything had been made ready for the thousands who would climb the mountain to the old Stanley homeplace on Memorial Day. Then Roy Lee had been killed. It would have been as good a time as any for Ralph to announce his retirement on the little stage in the hollow, not far from Carter's grave.

The Stanley Brothers had the most archaic sound of any bluegrass band. Ralph's banjo, while played in the fairly modern Scruggs-style, had the lost, lonesome sound of two hundred years of mountain life in its ring. His voice defied description: high, quiveringly poignant, a sound that was totally ageless in the essence of mountain mystique. The thought of his absence from the world of active bluegrass was almost unbearable.

The Clinch Mountain Boys were announced on stage at the Stanley Festival in May of 1974 and met thunderous applause. The fans were pleased and relieved to see the smiling face of Keith Whitley behind the guitar as the band broke into a rousing version of one of the old Mercury songs, "Nobody's Love Is Like Mine." Whitley's lead was easy and self-assured.

The sturdy mountain tenor reaching above the chorus was Ralph Stanley's, unchanged and irreplaceable. Hopefully, his sound of the mountains will live forever.

4

Flatt and Scruggs

"IF I WAS ON A FOGGY MOUNTAIN TOP"

Bill Monroe and his Blue Grass Boys were constantly on the road through 1946 and 1947. Roy Acuff might have been the king at the "Grand Ole Opry," but the word at WSM was that Bill Monroe was bringing in more personal appearance money than anyone.

The Blue Grass Boys worked hard at their music, as well as helping with the physical labor of pitching the big canvas show tent and participating in the exhibition baseball games that Monroe used as a "draw" before each show. Many tedious hours were spent in the long "stretch bus," with the boys sleeping, driving, or talking to pass the time and keep the driver from getting drowsy. Bill Monroe rode in the car with Lester Flatt; Bill's brother Birch, the bass player; and the fiddler, a smiling Floridian named Chubby Wise. Also in the car was the young man whose amazing banjo playing was causing such a stir in Nashville, a North Carolinian named Earl Scruggs.

During those long, hard drives through the mountains, the car radio was often tuned in to the broadcasts of Molly O'Day or Buddy Starcher. Mac Wiseman was a favorite down at WCYB, and he would later play an important part in the careers of Flatt, Scruggs, and Monroe himself. Bill's brother Charlie was a popular radio star. There were also a couple of brothers named Stanley from Virginia, and the popularity of their music showed Bill and the Boys that their style of music was good enough to warrant copying.

FLATT AND SCRUGGS

The dark-eyed, slightly built Earl Scruggs probably wondered what there was about his banjo playing that was causing such a commotion. The three-finger approach was widely used in his part of North Carolina, and Snuffy Jenkins had been playing the style professionally for years. Snuffy was, in fact, one of the major influences on Scruggs' banjo playing.

Actually, it was Earl's older brother Junie Scruggs who started him out in the style. Junie was one of the best around the little community of Flint Hill, in the western part of the state. Earl's father had played the banjo, but it was Junie who amazed young Earl with his ability to play a melody and surround it with so many notes.

North Carolina, it seemed, had always been known for its finger-style banjoists. Charlie Poole had grown up there and had taken his banjo and become one of the pioneer artists in the early country music field. He used the three-finger style and had done much to popularize the technique. Then there was Smith Hammet and the blind recording artist Mack Woolbright and Rex Brooks and a youngster named Johnny Whisnant.

Earl was impressed by all the great banjo music around him and began playing the old five-string that had belonged to his father before he could even reach the end of the neck. Before he reached his tenth birthday he was good enough to accompany his older brothers Junie and Horace over WSPA in Spartanburg, South Carolina.

By the time he was fifteen, he was accomplished enough to play with the professionals. It was 1939, and Earl was hired by one of the best groups in the Carolinas, the Morris Brothers. Wiley, George, and Zeke were a smooth singing group. Their fine harmony singing had enhanced some of the greatest string bands of the 1930s, and the combination of the breakdown fiddle band and good vocals laid the groundwork for the bluegrass-style bands that followed a decade later. When Earl joined them, the Morrises had the prime spot at WSPA, the early morning farm show.

The war years came, and the young banjo player went to work in the textile mills. Most of the young men from North Carolina had been called to the service, and those who were left at home found themselves working seventy-two-hour weeks. The grueling work and long hours made Earl realize that music would be a much better way of making a living. He went to Knoxville, one of Appalachia's musical Meccas, and took a job with an entertainer named "Lost" John Miller, who was scheduled to start a show from WSM.

"Lost" John Miller was heard by WSM's listeners every Saturday morning through the late summer and fall of 1945. Miller may have had high hopes of becoming an "Opry" star, but things didn't go too well, and by December he had decided to call it quits. The band had been commuting between Nashville and Knoxville, and Earl Scruggs was stranded away from home without a job.

But Earl had made friends in Nashville. His brilliant banjo playing had not gone unnoticed by the throng of musicians clustering around Bill Monroe. One of Earl's friends and admirers was an outstanding fiddler named Jimmy Shumate, who was then working with Monroe. He had been trying to get Earl to ask Monroe about a job, and now that Scruggs was free, an audition was arranged. Monroe liked what he heard, and Scruggs became a Blue Grass Boy the following Monday.

The impact made by this band on the whole field of traditional music is now legend. Chubby Wise soon replaced Shumate on fiddle, and Cedric Rainwater (Howard Watts) became the bassist in what was one of the greatest bands ever assembled, the band that was to become the definition of an entire style.

The Blue Grass Boys were seldom off the road in the two years that followed the addition of Scruggs to the Monroe lineup. It was a hard but rewarding way to make a living, the group members got along with one another, and Earl was developing a friendship with Lester Flatt, Monroe's guitar player and lead singer.

Flatt was an easygoing man in his thirties in that winter of 1945. He was raised near the eastern Tennessee town of Sparta, and he had sung in church and around the homeplace. He would sit and listen for hours as his father played the banjo and fiddle, and it wasn't long before young Lester was fooling around with the old five-string. His fine musical ear evidently told him that he wasn't destined to be a banjo player, and he soon switched to the guitar.

Like so many others in the mountains of the Southeast, Flatt was drawn immediately to the music of the Monroe Brothers. They had taken the familiar music of the hills, the music boys like Lester had been raised on, and added new life to it. Little did Lester realize that within a few years he himself would be playing with the Monroe Brothers—first with Charlie, then with Bill.

The good money and steady employment of the North Carolina textile industry drew Lester, as it had Earl Scruggs, into a mill job. And just like

Earl, Lester found the drudgery of the mill was helping him to decide upon music as his full-time occupation.

During his stay in North Carolina, Lester met and befriended a fine singer and guitarist named Clyde Moody. Moody had played and sung with the Mainers, and he later became one of Bill Monroe's finest lead singers. He was from the older school of guitarists who played rhythm with the thumb-and-finger pick—a style more related to the old "parlor" guitar styles than to the jazz-influenced playing of the Delmore Brothers and others. Both Maybelle Carter and Charlie Monroe used this thumb-and-finger technique, which involved playing the bass runs and melody notes with the thumb on the low strings while brushing a rhythm on the high strings with the first finger. This was the style at which Lester Flatt became adept. His playing lacked the melodic qualities of the Carters and the driving acrobatics of Monroe, but he was developing a smoothness and timing that were unbeatable. He was also learning to sing.

It was 1938 and Lester Flatt was well into his twenties before his guitar and singing became his means of support. He had become an accomplished performer by the early 1940s, and he and his wife, Gladys, were touring with one of the most popular bands of the South, Charlie Monroe and his Kentucky Pardners. Lester and Gladys (known professionally as Bobby Jean) sang as a duet on Charlie's stage and radio shows, and Lester became popular as a lead vocalist. But he was also singing a lot of the tenor with the elder Monroe brother, and his voice was getting higher and smoother. Like most of Charlie's tenors, Lester was singing his harmony much as Bill Monroe had done just a few years earlier, and this rounded his voice into fine shape for the next step in his career.

Flatt left the Kentucky Pardners in 1944, and he hadn't been away too long before he received the fateful telegram from Nashville. It was from Bill. Lester packed his bags and set off to make history.

He soon established himself as a vital part of the Blue Grass Boys. He emceed the shows and sang most of the lead, writing many of the songs and getting billing whenever the group was announced on the radio at WSM. He was a key figure on some of Monroe's biggest Columbia hits, but it wasn't until after the hiring of Scruggs that his role in the group became clearly defined and almost dominant.

Lester, Earl, and the others were touring with one of the star acts of the "Grand Ole Opry" and playing almost seven days a week. They were not unhappy, but it was a rough way to live. There was a tremendous amount of physical work expected of them, and there were those long drives on the winding mountain roads in the stretch bus, sleeping in a sitting position for several nights straight. Life on the road with Bill Monroe was as exhausting as it was exhilarating.

Lester and Earl had discussed quitting and striking out on their own. Lester wanted to play in the Knoxville area or perhaps join someone like Carl Story down in the Carolinas. But Earl was tired of the road and wanted to return to his home and the job at the textile mill. It was early in 1948 when Earl Scruggs quit Bill Monroe's band. Within weeks Flatt also gave his notice.

When Flatt and Scruggs left Bill Monroe, one of the greatest country bands ever assembled was broken up after four legendary years. They had created a style with their Columbia records that within a few short years had become the established standard for nearly all mountain string music. Their many followers were eager to see what Lester Flatt and Earl Scruggs would do on their own.

It didn't take much talking to convince Earl that the music world had more to offer than the cotton mill. He and Flatt began to get together to pick, and before long they were playing at Hickory, North Carolina, with Monroe alumni Jim Shumate and Cedric Rainwater. They moved to Bristol, and they had Mac Wiseman playing with them when they made their first recordings as Lester Flatt, Earl Scruggs, and the Foggy Mountain Boys for Mercury Records. They recorded four sides at a radio station in Knoxville in 1948, and these records proved beyond any doubt that they were a band to be reckoned with.

They recorded almost thirty sides for Mercury between 1948 and 1951, and these classic cuts became firmly established over the years as some of the finest bluegrass music ever recorded. Mac Wiseman sang tenor on the first few, Curly Sechler sang tenor on the others, and Lester's voice and Earl's fabulous banjo picking set for the musicians who were following the Bill Monroe pattern a standard that was perhaps even higher than that set by Monroe himself. The songs—recorded at various radio stations throughout the South—remain some of the most powerful bluegrass: "My Cabin in Caroline," "We'll Meet Again, Sweetheart," "Roll in My Sweet Baby's Arms," "Salty Dog Blues," "My Little Girl in Tennessee," the dazzling instrumentals "Farewell Blues" and "Pike County Breakdown," and the classic of them all "Foggy Mountain Breakdown."

FLATT AND SCRUGGS

Lester and Earl were probably not interested in outdoing Bill Monroe. After all, they had not really drawn that much from Monroe—they had added to Bill's ideas and helped formulate the sound that had become identified with him. They were playing the kind of music that they had been brought up with but that Monroe had congealed into a dynamic, commercial band style. They were generally more successful in capturing on record the drive and excitement of the new idiom, and Earl's banjo work was featured much more than it ever had been with Monroe's group. Lester's relaxed, ingratiating stage personality helped to give them an edge over the Monroe band that would put them more than a step ahead of the Blue Grass Boys for many years to come.

Almost from the first, Flatt and Scruggs sought to remove themselves from the nagging presence of the Bill Monroe image. They wanted to star in their own right, not to be known forever as Monroe's former sidemen. They seldom used the mandolin after the first few recording sessions, but in spite of this aversion to the Monroe tag, they were often compared with the Blue Grass Boys. This was due to the fact that the bands' styles were so similar, and that most of the early Foggy Mountain Boys had been members of the Blue Grass Boys: Cedric Rainwater, Jim Shumate, Mac Wiseman (who joined Monroe after leaving Flatt and Scruggs), Art Wooten, Benny Martin, Howdy Forrester, Chubby Wise, and others.

But the styles were only similar, not the same. Flatt and Scruggs had the drive, the good harmony singing, the exuberance. They had everything but that "high, lonesome" quality in which Monroe seemed to be losing himself after their departure. There was bitterness between the two bands and a competitive attitude was taking hold. As the unhealthy competition grew, there was an increasing reluctance to mention the name of the other group on stage or in publicity material.

Many older fans claim this was how the name "bluegrass" came to be used: Fans wanted to request some of the songs Flatt and Scruggs had done with Monroe but were afraid that mention of Bill's name would result in a negative response. The alternative to mentioning Monroe's name was to use the term *Blue Grass* or *bluegrass*.

Like most bands of the late 1940s, Lester and Earl and their group did a lot of station-hopping. They would move into an area and join the roster of the major local radio station, booking themselves into local schools and auditoriums, using the radio broadcasts as the means of publicizing their appearance dates. When their drawing power began to wane, they would move on to another area and another radio station—WROL and WNOX in Knoxville, WCYB in Bristol, WPTF in Raleigh—until their names were well known all over the mountain areas. They had established themselves as one of the top acts of the new "bluegrass" idiom, and by 1950 they found themselves negotiating contract terms with the label Monroe had just left. That same year saw the first Flatt and Scruggs releases on Columbia.

The groups Lester and Earl took with them into the recording studio during those early Columbia days were among the finest ever assembled. Mandolinist Curly Sechler's powerful tenor voice had become one of the characteristic sounds of the Flatt and Scruggs band, and their fiddlers were all of legendary stature: Benny Martin, Howdy Forrester, and Chubby Wise. On a few of the early Columbia sessions they were joined by a West Virginia mandolinist named Everett Lilly. Lilly's beautifully sweet tenor voice blended with Lester's on some of the best material of the early 1950s. But the foundation of the Flatt and Scruggs group was not in the sidemen but in the lilting, full-bodied voice of Lester Flatt and the brilliant, pounding banjo work of Earl Scruggs, heard to great advantage on the cuts of "Why Did You Wander?" "Come Back, Darlin'," "Get in Line, Brother," and the instrumentals "Earl's Breakdown" and "Flint Hill Special."

By the middle of the 1950s there was hardly a place in the entire Southeast where the music of Lester Flatt and Earl Scruggs wasn't known. They played the radio circuit from Bristol and Knoxville to Roanoke and Tampa, from Atlanta to Lexington. They were bringing in large crowds wherever they played, and their fame and popularity reached the attention of Cohen Williams, head of Martha White Mills, a Tennessee flour firm, who brought Flatt and Scruggs and their band to Nashville to host Martha White's early-morning radio spot at WSM.

The Martha White show was for many years the classic example of the early-morning country radio broadcast. Fifteen minutes in length, it featured great country music, much of which was never recorded commercially, and listeners felt as if the musicians were actually sitting there having a morning cup of coffee with them. There were the ever-present singing commercials, the good-natured banter with the announcer, sacred songs, fiddle tunes, and the announcing of show dates. The show was a success, and by 1955 Lester and Earl and their band were playing on the half-hour Martha White portion of the "Grand Ole Opry."

The sponsorship of the Martha White company was the best thing that could have happened to the band. Gone were the days of endless hustling for a week's work. They were on the Martha White payroll, and those checks were there every week, whether they worked or not. For a short time they were doing not only daily programs at WSM but also daily live programs from WRVA in Richmond and a station in Crewe, Virginia, as well as appearing on the WRVA "Old Dominion Barn Dance," making them one of the most listened-to acts in the South. But Martha White provided them with a tour bus and was getting them more than adequate bookings, and the other stations were dropped. Their road schedule was so exhausting that Martha White had to be talked into letting them tape all the morning radio shows in one day, allowing them more freedom to travel during the week. In addition to the radio broadcasts and personal appearances, they began doing television shows, appearing on several stations from Georgia up through the Carolinas to northern West Virginia. These programs were eventually taped in Nashville and syndicated.

There is little doubt that things were tense backstage at the "Opry." Monroe was still an "Opry" staple, and an enormous amount of jealousy existed between the two bands. Monroe, once one of the key stars of the "Opry," had fallen upon hard times. The mid-1950s were the low years for Bill. He had become more moody than ever, and the pain of an unsteady personal and professional life was showing in the increased "lonesomeness" of his music. He was paying his band union scale, and even then the paychecks were written only when the band worked. Flatt and Scruggs could pay their band a decent wage all year round and could keep the same musicians with them from year to year. Monroe could afford to pay little, and his often turbulent personal life made traveling with him an unenjoyable experience. Bill had always been terse and withdrawn, and his show appealed only to those who knew and understood him and his music, while Flatt and Scruggs had an extremely entertaining presentation that was a hit wherever they played.

The Blue Grass Boys and the Foggy Mountain Boys were being compared to each other less and less as the late 1950s approached. Flatt and Scruggs seemed to be doing their best to lose the Monroe sound. Curly Sechler was still carried as a singer, but the mandolin was hardly ever heard as a lead instrument. Another instrument was added to the group that took away much of the "hard" bluegrass sound. It was the dobro guitar, the acoustic Hawaiian-style instrument that had for many years been featured with the Roy Acuff band. From 1955 on the banjo was heard less and less, and the dobro began taking much of the instrumental load.

BLUEGRASS

There was a decided change in their music after the dobro was added. The early Columbia releases were done during their "hungry" days, the days when they still had to get out and hustle for their money. The music had guts and drive, qualities that may well have been just carryovers from the old Monroe influence. Their association with WSM and Martha White enabled them to pretty much take it easy. Their sound was becoming relaxed and comfortable, as opposed to soulful and powerful. Buck Graves, their dobroist, was a fine musician who had played with such names as Esco Hankins, Wilma Lee and Stoney Cooper, and Mac Wiseman. His greatness as an instrumentalist couldn't be denied, but his inclusion in the band resulted in a shift from the hard bluegrass sound, as heard on pre-dobro songs like "I'll Go Steppin' Too" and "Thinking of You," to a softer, hillbilly sound on such numbers as "On My Mind" and "Some Old Day."

Things were going well for Lester and Earl when country music plunged into a chaotic period following the advent of Elvis Presley and other rock 'n' roll hillbillies who brought a new sound to the southern market, a sound appropriately tagged "rockabilly." Country stars like Kitty Wells and the Louvin Brothers found themselves almost unable to withstand the changes that were occurring in the country music field. Many acts folded. Others went underground to wait for the storm to pass, not knowing if it ever would. The most traditional aspects of country music, as heard in the bluegrass bands, were the hardest hit of all. But even through the leanest years of country music, Flatt and Scruggs kept their noses above water. They were still selling a lot of cornmeal and wheat flour for Martha White, and the sponsorship of the Tennessee milling company gave Flatt and Scruggs something substantial to fall back on at a time when bands were given the choice of giving in to the changes or getting out of the business.

It was the end of a classic era for country music, but just when the situation seemed darkest for the bluegrass acts, something was happening in the field of popular music that proved to be a salvation for traditional music. The Kingston Trio (with their version of the North Carolina folk song "Tom Dooley"), the Limelighters, the Tarriers, and others were bringing a watered-down version of traditional folk music to eager audiences, and much of this new audience was anxious to learn what was behind America's great musical traditions. Black and white traditions alike began to be explored, and bluegrass was found to be a basically traditional style that was still being played commercially in the South. The folk music movement became a revival, and bluegrass, which had become even more of an embarrassment to country music when the rock movement emerged, found a new home among the colleges and coffeehouses of the North and West.

It was ironic that the respect the country and western field had hoped to gain by modernizing and diluting its sound was being bestowed upon the most blatantly "hillbilly" of all country music styles. The Osborne Brothers broke the college folk circuit barrier when they played the first bluegrass college date at Antioch College, Ohio, in 1959. Bluegrass became a standard element of the famed Newport Folk Festival, and hence, the numerous college folk festivals across the country. Artists like Earl Taylor, the Country Gentlemen, the Lilly Brothers, and Flatt and Scruggs found themselves playing in such esteemed concert halls as New York's Carnegie Hall.

The most farsighted bluegrass bands began seeing the tremendous potential of the folk music market, and Flatt and Scruggs, with the selling and promotional power of Columbia Records behind them, became a folk group. Their music didn't change that much, but Columbia saw the advantages of selling them to the ever-widening folk market as opposed to the traditionally narrow bluegrass market. Actually, Columbia had been trying to update Flatt and Scruggs' sound for several years, adding an occasional snare drum and echo effect. But folk music was tailor-made, and the early 1960s releases were primarily folk song collections that could be described as little more than "pleasant." A fine banjo instrumental album, "Foggy Mountain Banjo," came from that period, but everything they did after that was pretty much a reflection of what Columbia thought was going on in the folk music world.

Columbia recorded and released a collection of Flatt and Scruggs' versions of the folk-respectable Carter Family tunes, an excellent album that was enhanced by the presence of Mother Maybelle Carter and her autoharp. Next came a collection of standard folk tunes called "Folk Songs of Our Land," followed by a tepid mishmash of traditional Carter Family-Woody Guthrie tunes called "Hard Travelin'." That stage of their career was highlighted only by the release of two live albums, one recorded at Carnegie Hall, the other at Nashville's Vanderbilt University, both albums annotated gushingly by people who seemed to know nothing about other great bands in the business and were overly impressed by everything the Foggy Mountain Boys did.

It is hard to evaluate the music of Flatt and Scruggs during the early folk years. It was good music, well played and well sung. But it was low key, with a discernible lack of conviction. The band sounded tired and uncaring, the banjo work was predictable and uninspired, and Flatt's voice was being "echoed" almost beyond recognition.

Still, their records were selling. They were commanding top money on the folk music circuit, as some very slick press agentry praised them as the originators of the style—much to the dismay of Bill Monroe and his followers. Monroe's name, mentioned sparingly even during the early years, was never mentioned in the press releases as Lester and Earl moved rapidly to the top. The word *bluegrass* was evasively defined on one set of Flatt and Scruggs jacket notes as "A polite pseudonym for 'hillbilly,'" and several published interviews with Mrs. Earl Scruggs gave the whole story of bluegrass in terms of Flatt and Scruggs, not once mentioning the name of Bill Monroe.

Folk music continued to grow, and it was beginning to be used in movies and television shows. One such show was "The Beverly Hillbillies," a spoof of the plight of country people moved to the big city. The show's name derived from a popular radio group of the 1930s, and its general format was drawn from the likes of the old Weaver Family and Ma and Pa Kettle films. Important to bluegrass was the fact that the group chosen to do "The Beverly Hillbillies" theme music was Lester Flatt, Earl Scruggs, and the Foggy Mountain Boys.

The show became the hit of the season, and the theme was one of Columbia's big sellers of the mid-1960s. The banjo market skyrocketed, and many Nashville recordings began coming out with the plinky, sparkling sound of the bluegrass banjo—a sound that Nashville had shunned for years as being too corny. The success of the program was more than likely bolstered by the musical success of Flatt and Scruggs' "The Ballad of Jed Clampett," and so much were Lester and Earl identified with the program that they became semi-regulars on the weekly situation comedy.

Flatt and Scruggs' drawing power during the early 1960s far overshadowed that of any other bluegrass act. Whenever a bluegrass band was needed to round out a folk music show, Flatt and Scruggs usually got the job—and usually at a price double or triple that of any other good bluegrass band, even those of Monroe or the Stanley Brothers. The once-great Foggy Mountain Boys' bluegrass sound became increasingly folk-oriented, and Lester and Earl themselves seemed to be less and less interested in the kind of music they were being encouraged to play. Disappointment was felt by the people who had supported them and bought their records in the days when hardly anyone was paying any attention to bluegrass music.

Columbia Records, like any large commercial company, was interested in one thing: turning out a product it felt could sell. Columbia was evidently selling more records using the new Flatt and Scruggs formula than they had back in the early days, and the new releases seemed to get slicker and slicker as album after album was pushed on the market. High-powered session artists like guitarist Grady Martin and harmonica man Charlie McCoy were added to the recordings. This was a departure from the standard bluegrass practice of not using gimmicks or "ringers" (musicians other than those used in stage shows) in recording work. Columbia hired several musicians for its Flatt and Scruggs sessions who had never even played bluegrass, a device intended to give the sound a commercial fullness. The actual result was to detract from the featured musicians (in whom Columbia seemingly had little personal confidence) and give the total sound an overproduced, cluttered effect. Columbia was pushing Johnny Cash material on them, and the success of "Jed Clampett" prompted the release of bland versions of even blander TV numbers like "Green Acres" and "Petticoat Junction."

The national taste for folk music had probably given birth to the "Beverly Hillbillies" concept, and hence Flatt and Scruggs' participation in the popular Hollywood venture. Folk music was riding high in 1963, and Flatt and Scruggs were on the crest of the wave. But new waves were being felt in the music world, and they were coming from the direction of the British Isles. The Beatles jumped on the scene with a full-grown music movement—British rock. Folk music had been pushed to its limits with the "hootenanny" craze. The music world was ready for something new, and the Beatles were there with the right product at the right time.

The Beatles were an extension of the rock movement; some of the early recordings of the British quartet ("Twist and Shout," "Roll Over, Beethoven," and "Matchbox"), as well as those of the Rolling Stones, are virtually indistinguishable from their American counterparts. But whereas the rock and folk music movements existed pretty much on equal ground in the late 1950s and early 1960s, the advent of British rock kicked the last vestiges of life out of commercial folk music. The folk music craze, like the postwar country music field before it, died a premature death in the wake of the ever-loudening sound of rock 'n' roll. Like the country musicians less than a decade before them, the folk artists saw that they would either have to change their style or perish in the competitive commercial music market.

BLUEGRASS

Styles were changed, to be sure, and the American answer to the British takeover in popular music was a new style—a mixture of the folk sound and the rock sound: folk-rock.

Folk music came to an almost immediate halt, and the bluegrass bands again found themselves in the painful position of being left without a larger, more commercial style to which they could attach themselves. Nashville had long given up trying to sell bluegrass to the mass audience, and Nashville's Country Music Association (organized by the country music hierarchy in 1958) barely recognized the fact that bluegrass existed—it was too embarrassingly country to fit their new, slick, modernized approach. While some of the other big-name bluegrass groups were still enjoying small but steady record sales, only Lester Flatt and Earl Scruggs were really making good money playing acoustic country music.

The Beatles and their far-reaching impact on the music world didn't have much of an effect on a country music industry that was just beginning to revive itself from the post-Elvis slump. Sounds of rock were beginning to be heard in country recordings, but the approval of country music by groups like the Beatles and the Lovin' Spoonful were more of a boon to country music than anything else. But where did that leave Flatt and Scruggs? They were no longer bluegrass, and their woefully inept versions of Bob Dylan's tunes even took them out of the country camp. They were not country, not bluegrass, and if they were a folk-rock band, then they were a very poor one. The band was unhappy and obviously going stale. Flatt, one of the greatest of all bluegrass singers, sounded foolish trying to sing Dylan songs like "Rainy Day Woman" and "Tambourine Man," which he probably didn't even like. And the great Earl Scruggs, whose phenomenal banjo playing once brought "Opry" audiences to their feet, had lost almost everything but the fantastic timing. Missed notes and mistakes became an expected part of his performance, and the 1965 rerecording of his "Foggy Mountain Breakdown" was a sad, sluggish ghost of the classic version of only fifteen years before.

The one bright spot of their mid-1960s output was the LP they cut with Doc Watson, the legendary blind guitar wizard from North Carolina. The album was called "Strictly Instrumental" and was notable principally for the outstanding lead guitar work by Watson. If Lester Flatt was even at the session, his guitar was either channeled out or drowned out by three or four other guitarists. Scruggs' banjo playing was better than usual, and the Foggy Mountain Boys' Paul Warren on fiddle and Buck Graves on dobro did their usual great jobs. But the album had the same overproduced sound that had become the Columbia trademark, and the session was almost ruined by the presence of harmonica player Charlie McCoy, who faked his way through almost every number, displaying an almost complete ignorance of the material and the idiom.

Financially they still did well under the push and protectivism of Columbia Records. But their biggest success of the mid-1960s may also have had something to do with their eventual undoing. Again, Hollywood was behind it, having found that bluegrass music was indeed the best thing going when a rural mood needed to be created. In 1967 a film was made about the lives and times of the legendary southwestern bank robbers Bonnie Parker and Clyde Barrow. The film included some highly energetic chase sequences through the fields of the Midwest, and an old record was found that combined the mood of an exciting chase with the images of old cars, rut-filled roads, and rickety old barns. The movie producer's fortuitous find was the original 1950 recording of Flatt and Scruggs' "Foggy Mountain Breakdown."

Bonnie and Clyde was the sensation of the 1967 movie season, and everyone got on the bandwagon. Several popular songs were written about them, the Bonnie-and-Clyde look was the rage in the fashion world, and scores of commercials were produced with a 1930s gangster theme, complete with bluegrass banjo. Not only did the film win top honors that year, but the old record—fully eighteen years after its original release—won honors in the recording industry, almost as if it had been recorded especially for the film.

Lester and Earl quickly jumped on their own bandwagon with a Columbia "Bonnie and Clyde" album, comprising songs written especially for the LP with a Barrow and Parker theme. This record marked the recording debut of Earl's son, Randy, a budding young Watson-style guitarist. The album also marked yet another attempt to rerecord the "Foggy Mountain Breakdown." Recording this tune again, especially at a time when the great original performance was being so widely heard, can only be seen as very poor judgment on someone's part. Earl Scruggs 1968 was competing with Earl Scruggs 1950, and the competition was just too stiff; it showed that Earl was a tired man whose playing had lost much of the fire it had once had. Playing the two versions of this great banjo showpiece back to back is a telling experience.

New doors were opened to Lester and Earl after the film became a hit. But they seemed just too tired and fed up with the whole thing to do very much about it. There was trouble in the ranks, probably caused by the manner in which the band was being managed. Another of Scruggs' sons, Gary, was being pushed into the act. They were, at one time, carrying four rhythm guitarists: the two Scruggs boys, country music veteran Johnnie Johnson, and Lester. It was clear to some that Lester Flatt was being forced to take a back seat to the Scruggs family.

They were never more well known than in 1969, when an item appeared in the press. It was from Nashville, where an announcement had been made that one of the most durable teams in country music, Lester Flatt and Earl Scruggs, had broken up. Two new bands were then heard as "Grand Ole Opry" regulars: Lester Flatt and the Nashville Grass and the Earl Scruggs Review.

The extent to which Flatt and Scruggs were pulling in opposite directions was no more evident than in the sounds of their respective bands after they parted. The Scruggs band became essentially a country rock band with a five-string banjo. Randy Scruggs played some outstanding acoustic and electric lead guitar while his older brother, Gary, played electric bass and sang in a semi-rock style. The group also included a full set of drums. Earl was still playing much as he had for thirty years, but he seemed to be much more at ease playing with his family than he had in the last years with Lester Flatt. The group continued to record for Columbia and by the mid-1970s seemed to have arrived at a workable hybrid of bluegrass, country music, and rock.

Lester Flatt, much to the delight and relief of the bluegrass world, went back to the same style he had played in the 1950s, but with the commercial savvy he had accumulated from being in the upper echelons of popular music. When the Foggy Mountain Boys broke up, most members of the band (Paul Warren, Buck Graves, and bassist Jake Tullock) chose to stay with Lester, probably because of those weekly checks from Martha White, with whom Lester remained under contract. Flatt kept the early-morning radio show at WSM—one of the last of the dying breed of live country radio broadcasts—as well as the Martha White spot on the "Grand Ole Opry."

Lester's Nashville Grass (a name arrived at after a write-in contest was held on their radio show) soon included two of the best young bluegrass musicians, both of whom had just completed a successful stretch with Bill Monroe: mandolinist Roland White and banjoist Vic Jordan. They were playing solid bluegrass again, and their appearance at the major bluegrass festivals was welcomed by thousands of fans who thought Lester Flatt was lost forever as an active bluegrass musician.

The Lester Flatt group recorded one last LP with Columbia called "Flatt Out." It had some good music on it, which couldn't be heard over the aggressive rock drums, overdubbed after Flatt and the group left the studio. Lester was never to record for Columbia again. It was soon announced that he had signed with RCA.

RCA Records' man in Nashville is the great guitarist Chet Atkins, a sensitive musician and an equally sensitive artist and repertoire man. He doesn't guess the market for a certain product—he knows and he takes it from there. Atkins knew when he hired Flatt that there was a market for his music, a large number of people who stopped buying his records when he stopped recording the kind of music they liked to hear. He knew also that the kind of record buyers who bought and liked the later Flatt and Scruggs material would probably continue to buy the Columbia stuff that Scruggs and his sons were recording. So Lester was with a label that knew what the fans of Lester Flatt wanted: Lester Flatt in a bluegrass context. RCA was more than successful in capturing the new, easygoing Lester Flatt bluegrass sound and even undertook a project to reunite Flatt with one of his old singing partners, Mac Wiseman. Wiseman had been one of Lester and Earl's first tenor singers, and had gone on to bluegrass and country stardom both as a performer and businessman. He became an executive with Dot Records in the 1950s and had signed with RCA shortly before Lester left Columbia.

The reunion of the two great bluegrass singers in a totally bluegrass context proved to be one of the best things to happen on major-label bluegrass for some time. The records were some of RCA's big sellers of the early 1970s—at least one of the three "Lester 'n' Mac" LPs graced the national record charts.

With the darkest part of their careers past and almost forgotten, it is now possible to take an honest look at the music of Lester Flatt and Earl Scruggs. To begin with, they were the most widely heard and warmly received bluegrass-style band of them all. They took bluegrass to places where it otherwise would never have been heard, and their roles as popularizers of the bluegrass style can't be overstated.

Earl Scruggs' contribution to the sound of bluegrass music is probably the single most important element in explaining or summarizing any popularity bluegrass may have enjoyed over the past thirty years. Of the three or four bluegrass-style songs that have reached national "hit" levels, two can be accredited to Earl Scruggs: "The Ballad of Jed Clampett" and "Foggy Mountain Breakdown." The rising stature of bluegrass music in the late 1960s may be attributed directly to these two numbers.

Their recorded work, especially their recordings made between the time they left Bill Monroe and the time when Columbia began taking them out of bluegrass, is probably the most important body of recorded bluegrass in the entire field. Opinions may vary on the validity of the music they made in their last years together, and unfavorable comparisons may be drawn between the two groups they formed after separating, but for an honest appraisal of their greatness we must look to the effect of the early Flatt and Scruggs group on the bluegrass of today.

One glance at a list of songs from any amateur band will probably reveal more Flatt and Scruggs songs than anything else. This is the gauge of their influence on the great music style. The names of Lester Flatt and Earl Scruggs will be remembered as long as bluegrass music is played.

5

Don Reno and Red Smiley

INNOVATIONS

One day in Spartanburg, South Carolina, during World War II, Bill Monroe and his Blue Grass Boys (Clyde Moody, Chubby Wise, and "Cousin" Wilbur Westbrook) came to town to perform over radio station WSPA.

The radio station had its own banjo player, a skinny kid with ears that stuck out and shoulders barely wide enough to support a banjo strap. The kid's name was Don Reno.

As sometimes happens when country musicians come to town, Monroe hosted a jam session at the hotel where he was staying. It was a classic—the first time Monroe had ever heard a three-finger banjo picker play with his group. Monroe was enthralled. There was nothing the young Reno couldn't play—breakdowns, gospel tunes, ballads, blues, waltzes. Monroe excitedly told Moody he had found the sound he had been looking for, and he offered Reno a job with the Blue Grass Boys.

Reno told Monroe he had enlisted in the army but still had to take the physical exam. If he couldn't pass the physical, Reno told Monroe, he'd take the job.

Reno turned out to be physically fit, and Monroe lost a banjo player.

By the time Don Reno was discharged from the army, Earl Scruggs had joined Monroe's band, and his fiery banjo playing was bringing down the house at the old Ryan Auditorium in Nashville. Scruggs became an instant hit, and the style became known as the Scruggs-style of banjo playing. But if it hadn't been for a doctor's stethoscope, thousands of banjoists would be playing Reno-style today.

What Don Reno didn't know was that within a little more than a decade after his discharge from the army he would be known as the greatest five-string banjo player in the country.

Don Reno is a legend in bluegrass music. He has been at the center of banjo-playing controversy almost since he first appeared in public. Many don't like his distinctive style; thousands of others love it. One thing can't be denied: The records Reno made with his rich-voiced partner, the late Red Smiley, are some of the greatest ever recorded in the bluegrass field.

Spartanburg is Don's home, and he started his professional career there at the age of twelve, playing the harmonica and guitar at WSPA. The banjo playing of Snuffy Jenkins was instrumental in Reno's switch from guitar to the five-string banjo.

Nearly every banjoist from the "first generation" of bluegrass pickers (those born before the Depression) cites DeWitt "Snuffy" Jenkins as his principal inspiration. Most banjo players in the 1930s used the old frailing or clawhammer style. But Snuffy had a style that used metal finger picks on the thumb and first two fingers of the right hand. This enabled him to play melody on a variety of tunes where the banjo could ordinarily play only backup. Snuffy was playing with J. E. Mainer when Don Reno first heard him. The Mainer group played in a style that was close to early bluegrass, and it was this sound that Monroe was trying to emulate when he hired his first banjo player in 1942. The Morris Brothers (Zeke, Wiley, and George) were a part of many of the early bands, and young Reno was discovered by Zeke and George at radio station WISE in Ashville, North Carolina.

The Morrises took Reno to WSPA, and it was there he met and joined a talented multi-instrumentalist named Arthur Smith. Their association lasted well into the 1950s. Together they recorded Smith's big hit of the era, "Guitar Boogie." Much later they recorded a tune called "Feudin' Banjos," which was borrowed by Warner Brothers Records some twenty years later for the movie *Deliverance* and caused a minor stir and several legal headaches for those who failed to give credit to Reno and Smith.

Reno loved the music of the Blue Grass Boys and was thrilled to jam with Bill Monroe that day in the Spartanburg hotel room. He was bitterly disappointed when Earl Scruggs beat him to the limelight at the "Grand Ole Opry."

Reno had returned from the war and had rejoined Arthur Smith. Smith's

"Guitar Boogie" hit was little consolation for the painful fact that Scruggs, not Reno, was the star on the "Opry." It was clear that the Carolina style of banjo playing would forever be identified with Scruggs. But Reno was determined to insure that he would not be known as an imitator of Earl Scruggs.

In 1948, five years after Reno and Monroe first played together, Earl Scruggs left the Monroe band. Reno, determined not to miss the second chance, packed his banjo and headed out across the mountains toward Nashville. When he got there, he learned that Monroe was on tour in the Carolinas, so he jumped in the car and started back the way he had come. Bill and the Blue Grass Boys were playing one of the little towns in North Carolina when Don caught up with them. As Reno tells it, he tuned up while Monroe was on stage, walked out unannounced, and joined in. Even Bill Monroe was surprised.

The loss of Earl Scruggs and Lester Flatt in 1948 hurt Monroe and his music, and he had to work his new men even harder to get his show back into shape. Reno was a tremendous help. He could double on guitar and banjo and sing any harmony part. Monroe went through two or three guitar players before he hired Mac Wiseman in 1949, and it was Wiseman who was with him when he went into the studio to record his last sides for Columbia that same year. But by that time Reno had moved on.

Don Reno returned to the Carolinas, joining Tommy Magness and the Tennessee Buddies. Magness had been one of Monroe's great early fiddlers and was fresh from the Roy Acuff band when he contacted Reno in late 1949. The guitarist in the Magness band was a tall redhead named Arthur Lee Smiley.

The Carolinas have often been called the true cradle of bluegrass music because of their wealth of great musicians. One of the greatest was Red Smiley, a native of Ashville, North Carolina.

Red was born into an educated family. His father was a school teacher and a friend of the late Bascom Lamar Lunsford, the great old-time banjo player and founder of the famed Ashville Folk Festival. The music of the early duets made an impression on young Red, and by the late 1930s he was playing over WROL in Knoxville. He seemed destined even then, at the age of thirteen, to be a professional musician.

But Red was called into the army in 1942. He was critically wounded in Sicily when bomb fragments tore through his chest. Red spent more than two years in army hospitals and finally lost his left lung.

BLUEGRASS

If the loss of the lung left Smiley with any psychological scars, they weren't evident in his singing voice. He was singing to fellow patients while still in the Walter Reed Memorial Hospital and lost no time in returning to music in North Carolina. In 1946 he joined a band that featured two of the musicians who were to be associated with Red Smiley and Don Reno for many years: fiddler Jimmy Lunsford and mandolinist Red Rector.

Bluegrass music was just catching the ear of the rural South as the 1940s came to a close. Smiley had moved to Ohio by then, heading a band as a straight country singer. His solid, bluegrass guitar style and pure country voice seemed even better suited to the traditional styles, and when Tommy Magness offered him a job, Red joined him at WDBJ in Roanoke. There he met Don Reno. Reno was a great banjo player, Smiley was a great guitar player, and their voices couldn't have been better matched. They knew they were meant to be a team.

Don and Red left the Tennessee Buddies to play with Toby Stroud at 50,000-watt WWVA in Wheeling, West Virginia. Stroud played a combination of straight country and bluegrass, sometimes carrying two sets of musicians: a bluegrass band and a country band. Reno and Smiley tired of this arrangement and left Stroud in 1952 but had acquired enough confidence to strike out on their own. It was obvious to Syd Nathan, then head of King Records, that Reno and Smiley had something that could probably sell a lot of records. He lost no time signing them to a contract.

King was an important label of the postwar years; it had the Delmore Brothers, Grandpa Jones, Clyde Moody, Cowboy Copas, Hawkshaw Hawkins, and several other important names. Syd Nathan was looking for a bluegrass band in 1952.

It seemed to be the thing in those days—every major label had at least one bluegrass band on the payroll. Monroe was at Decca; the Stanleys were at Columbia and would soon join Mercury; Flatt and Scruggs were at Mercury and would soon join Columbia; the Lonesome Pine Fiddlers were at RCA. Nathan had hopes of hitting the then-new bluegrass market when he recorded the classic few cuts by Jimmy Martin and Bob Osborne in 1951, but things didn't seem to work out. Most of the backup group consisted of the Lonesome Pine Fiddlers, and shortly after the records were cut Osborne was drafted into the marines and Jimmy Martin returned to play with Bill Monroe.

Nathan signed Don Reno and Red Smiley and their band, the Tennessee Cut-Ups. The group included Red's old friends Jimmy Lunsford and Red Rector as well as the legendary bluegrass bassist John Palmer.

King was doing well in the gospel market with various quartet groups (usually including people like the Delmores and Grandpa Jones), and it was decided that Don and Red would record some religious material. The result was some superior bluegrass gospel, sixteen cuts of excellent music on which Reno sang a variety of parts and played not only banjo but lead guitar and some remarkable finger-picked mandolin. Many of the songs were Reno's own compositions, and these stand as some of the very finest material ever done in bluegrass: "Get Behind Me, Satan," "The Lord's Last Supper," and the best known of the early King material, "I'm Using my Bible for a Road Map."

"Road Map" was a big seller for King, but ironically, the group just couldn't make a go of it on the road. Their career had just begun when they had to make the painful decision to disband.

Reno returned to Arthur Smith and in 1954 helped Smith record the original "Feudin' Banjos." The number featured Reno on the five-string and Smith on the tenor banjo in a simulated duel for musical supremacy. This classic cut, recorded and released on the MGM label, is still musically interesting after twenty years, better than the many versions that followed it under the title "Duelin' Banjos."

King continued to record and release the music of Don Reno and Red Smiley, even though they weren't really a band anymore. The recordings made during that period are some of the best: "Springtime in Dear Old Dixie," "Talk of the Town," "Dixie Breakdown," "I Know You're Married, But I Love You Still," "Charlotte Breakdown," and many others.

The sound Reno and Smiley were developing through the early 1950s was totally different from that recorded by Monroe and the others. They seemed to be aiming at a different market. That era in country music was marked by the switchover to electric instruments. Drums hadn't yet found their way to Nashville, but songs were geared more and more to the honky-tonk crowd, songs about honky-tonk angels, cheatin' hearts, neon signs that flashed into sleazy motel room windows, and the problems encountered by hillbillies moving into urban culture. Hank Williams and Ernest Tubb were the kings of the barroom tear-jerker, as fans in country music roadhouses all over the country danced and drank to songs like Tubb's "Walkin' the Floor over You," and Williams' "Honky Tonkin'," "Hey, Good Lookin'," and the classic "Your Cheatin' Heart."

This was the music Red Smiley had been performing as a featured country vocalist in Ohio. Now Reno and Smiley were turning it into bluegrass, and it sounded great. They both had enough show business savvy to know that not everyone was going to identify with songs about cabins in the hills, so they added a dance-floor beat to their music and began singing dance-type country tunes like "One Teardrop and One Step Away." They had more than enough talent and ability to pull it off. Red had the most appealingly commercial voice in bluegrass, and Reno's smooth tenor blended with it perfectly. In addition, Reno was an extremely sophisticated musician, able to play an imaginative banjo break on anything. He added elements of electric and steel guitar technique to his banjo work. On the slower tunes, his full-chordal style, almost like plectrum banjo playing, added an entirely new dimension to bluegrass five-string banjo.

Reno was considered the best writer of new, original bluegrass tunes through most of his career, and the majority of the top songs recorded by Reno and Smiley in their heyday were Don Reno compositions.

The King records sold well through the early 1950s—so well, in fact, that requests for personal appearances began coming on a basis regular enough to cause them to reorganize. For their reactivation they hired their old friend bassist John Palmer. A good show fiddler was needed, and Mack Magaha got the job in 1955. This band stayed together for many years and is remembered as the classic vintage of the Tennessee Cut-Ups.

One of the most important Saturday night radio "jamborees" was the "Old Dominion Barn Dance," broadcast from powerful WRVA in Richmond, Virginia. Like WWVA in Wheeling, the beam went all over the Northeast, bringing the sound of country music to a huge audience. Mac Wiseman was a regular, as were Flatt and Scruggs. In 1955 the premier bluegrass act of the "Barn Dance" was the Reno and Smiley group. They also secured an important spot on television, the "Top o' the Morning" show at WDBJ-TV in Roanoke. They were getting more television and radio exposure than any group outside Nashville.

In the time of their greatest popularity, the Tennessee Cut-Ups were considered the greatest show band ever assembled in the field of bluegrass. Not only did they exhibit vocal and instrumental superiority, but they were polished and capable showmen. Other musicians could play flashy licks all day long and never really reach the crowd. Reno and Magaha made listeners know they were hearing something special, made them sit up, pay attention, and love what they were hearing.

Not the least of their stage appeal was their great country comedy. They would stage elaborate skits, using ridiculous hillbilly outfits and names like Chicken and Pansy Hotrod (Don and Red), Mutt Highpockets (Palmer), and Jeff Dooly Tater (Magaha). The riotous routines would sometimes last ten or fifteen minutes, and it was the kind of comedy the country audiences couldn't get enough of.

It was largely their comedy that made them unique in bluegrass music through the late 1950s. Monroe and most of the others were already aware that bluegrass was developing its own audience and had gone "serious," feeling that they no longer had to sell a product to a large, general market. Bluegrass musicians, following the lead established by Monroe, became known as sullen, dour-faced individuals who would rarely laugh, smile, joke, or give any indication of enjoying what they were doing. Most bluegrass bands relegated their comedy to the bass player, and even that tradition was eventually dropped as the country market became more sophisticated. But Reno and Smiley were determined to give folks an enjoyable, entertaining performance for their money, and that's exactly what they did.

They were stylists, showmen, songwriters. But the most lasting contribution of the Reno and Smiley sound to the ever-broadening field of bluegrass was the phenomenal banjo playing of Don Reno. His active mind restlessly searched for something new. New licks and songs seemed to pour out of him, and he was, without question, the most creative and imaginative instrumentalist of the years before 1960. He was a musician's musician, his left hand all over the fingerboard as his right hand executed roll after endless roll. It was improvisational playing, and his complete knowledge of the instrument and fertile imagination produced sounds that ranged from dazzling to unbelievable. Reno and his school of jazzy, spontaneous bluegrass banjo playing was responsible for the eventual elevation of the idiom to the status once enjoyed only by classical music and jazz. It started an upward trend in bluegrass that still thrives.

Almost every banjo tune Reno did became standard fare for the many flashy banjo players coming into their own, especially after the folk music revival brought the five-string banjo into the limelight after years of obscurity. The Reno tunes were the essence of instrumental showiness, and numbers like "Little Rock Getaway," "Double Banjo Blues," and "Dixie Breakdown" became standard bluegrass showpieces.

Reno and Smiley and their band were among the fortunate ones. The daily television show in Roanoke was steady employment and enabled them to keep the same musicians year after year. It meant they didn't have to be on the road continually to make their living. The "Old Dominion Barn

Dance" spread their name across most of the East, and their King records were being widely distributed and sold. Then, at the zenith, the act broke up.

The bluegrass world was shaken by the news that one of its best-loved acts would no longer be making the circuit. Reasons were sought for the breakup, and gossip-hungry insiders were disappointed to learn that the two men parted friends. The "Old Dominion Barn Dance" had closed its doors in 1964, depriving them of one of their principal means of exposure. An attempt to revive the program on television was unsuccessful, and Reno felt a need to take his music to wider markets and new territory. Smiley, in failing health, was unable to go along with it. It was an amiable parting, and they would eventually reunite, but the glory days of the old Reno and Smiley bands were over.

An earnest desire to stay in the business ruled out early retirement for both men. They formed bands that were among the best of the late 1960s. Smiley kept the "Top o' the Morning" TV show in Roanoke, organizing a group that included banjoist David Deese, tenor singer Gene Burrows, veteran fiddler Clarence "Tater" Tate, and the faithful John Palmer on bass. Reno joined forces with the great fiddler Benny Martin but was soon to form an outstanding group with singer Bill Harrell. Reno and Harrell kept the name Tennessee Cut-Ups, though neither is from Tennessee, and Smiley called his band, appropriately, the Bluegrass Cut-Ups.

Comparisons between the two groups were inevitable, as they became staple attractions of the new bluegrass festivals springing up in the South. Both bands were outstanding, with the Reno band leaning more toward the old Reno and Smiley sound—smooth duets, fancy banjo licks and all. The Smiley group was the smoother (if less creative) of the two and featured a more solid, or hard, bluegrass sound, especially after banjoist Deese was replaced by the super-solid Billy Edwards. Both bands recorded extensively for several labels, including Rural Rhythm, Cabin Creek, Rimrock, Rome, and, of course, King.

Reno and Smiley aged remarkably in the few short years they were apart. Red, already thin, became almost skeletal as his health declined. Reno's hair, which had always been dark, turned white and he seemed to be gaining the weight Smiley was losing. Both bands had problems. Reno and Harrell seemed to be having trouble arriving at a unified sound as musicians came and went from their band. Reno's son Ronnie played mandolin for a time. Veteran George Shuffler played bass and lead guitar, then left to rejoin Ralph Stanley. Finally a good sound was found with the additions of fiddler Buck Ryan and bassist Jerry McCoury.

DON RENO AND RED SMILEY

Red Smiley's television show at Roanoke was canceled in 1969. His health forced him to retire. But Red couldn't stay away and was soon a feature of several of the bluegrass festivals, where Reno and Smiley reunions were becoming almost too predictable. Predictable also was the announcement that Smiley was coming out of retirement as a featured part of the Reno and Harrell band. A couple of very listenable LPs were released in the early 1970s, and they were again touring together extensively when Red suffered a series of mild heart attacks. Refusing to slow down, he was more shockingly thin and ill-looking at each appearance, although his standard of performance was as high as ever. He was taken ill during a flu epidemic in late 1971, an illness from which he never recovered.

Red Smiley died in the first few days of the new year, 1972. He was one of the finest singers, guitarists, and performers the bluegrass field had known. A warm and genial personality on stage and off, Red was widely mourned in a field still so young that the deaths of the founders are rare and carry a tremendous impact of disbelief. Still, to those who saw Red in the last years of his life, the news of his passing came as no shock.

The Reno and Harrell band continues to be active, although Don Reno has reportedly not been in the best of health. But he still knows more about the neck of the five-string banjo than anyone, even though his true greatness isn't in what he does today but in the creative genius he brought to bluegrass and the banjo fifteen and twenty years ago. He made a lasting impression on a music style that was then still young and impressionable. Reno and Smiley were one of the most widely recorded bands in the music's thirty-year history, and their legacy is one of change, sophistication, and tasteful innovation.

At the Berryville bluegrass festival in the summer of 1968, promoter Carlton Haney staged one of his famous festival firsts. Reno and Harrell had been booked, as had Smiley's Bluegrass Cut-Ups. The Osborne Brothers were there, too, with Don's son Ronnie on electric bass—he had been the Tennessee Cut-Ups' mandolin player since before he was tall enough to reach a microphone. Haney had also booked the Porter Wagoner band, not a bluegrass group but they had with them the amazing, jumping Mack Magaha on fiddle. A full-blown reunion was held: Reno, Smiley, John Palmer, Ronnie Reno, and Mack Magaha. They had lost none of the magic, and it was pure electricity, not nostalgia, that brought the audience to it's feet with a roar that was probably heard for ten miles in every direction.

6

Jimmy Martin

ON THE SUNNY SIDE
OF THE MOUNTAIN

We are sitting on apple crates under several scraggly beech trees at a bluegrass festival in Virginia. A good band has just left the stage, and the appreciative audience gives them a warm ovation that is something less than a call for an encore. A local DJ, acting as master of ceremonies, walks up to the mike. He glances at his watch and looks at the next act listed on his roster. The audience grows quiet. Some check their folded programs, but the emcee has beat them to it by announcing that the next act is Jimmy Martin and the Sunny Mountain Boys.

A few in the audience don't know Jimmy Martin from Dean Martin. Others know him from his performance on the Nitty Gritty Dirt Band's monumental "Will the Circle Be Unbroken?" album. Most of us know who Jimmy Martin is, and the announcement of his name is met with a roar of approval that makes the ovation given the previous band seem pale by comparison.

Hardly anyone is fully prepared for Jimmy Martin, even if they've seen him before. The applause is still thunderous as the Sunny Mountain Boys run—not walk—to center stage. The first thing that catches the eye is a little man in the gaudiest gold lamé paisley jacket imaginable. He's wearing cranberry bellbottoms, snow-white slippers, and jauntily perched on his head is a pink satin brocade cowboy hat. He waves as he prances, flashing a broad, cocky smile, and around his middle hangs a beautiful, pearl-inlaid

Martin guitar with a name emblazoned down the fingerboard. The name, of course, is Jimmy Martin.

The big guitar is hefted up to a nearby microphone and a distinctive takeoff on the famous Lester Flatt "G run" is flawlessly executed. Jimmy has done such a good job of capturing our attention that we've hardly noticed the four musicians on stage with him. Now the banjo player cuts down on some of the fastest, hardest banjo playing we've heard all day. The banjo pounds on, an electric bass thumps a tubalike rhythm, and Jimmy Martin whoops, whistles, jumps, shouts, and goads the audience into applauding the struggling banjoist, who seems in danger of being overpowered by the strutting little guitarist. Then Martin steps up to the microphone, very close, and starts to sing:

"My Sophronie's from Kentucky, now she's found another man.
I can't even kiss her, can't even hold her hand. . . ."

It's a loud voice. Unmistakably, it's a bluegrass voice, although there's nothing lonesome about it. It's brassy, country, exciting. Swagger, war whoops, and gold lamé aside, we are listening to what has been called the greatest bluegrass lead voice in the world.

The story begins in a place called Sneedville. No kidding. It's in the mountains of eastern Tennessee, near Kingsport. Jimmy Martin was born there and learned to play an old, cheap guitar between his farm chores. He sang in church. His stepfather was, in fact, the local singing teacher. The "Grand Ole Opry" was tuned in every Saturday night (Jimmy later recorded a song about it), and Bill Monroe left his forceful impression on the young Tennessean. Jimmy dreamed of the day when he might be able to go to Nashville and sing with Monroe on the "Opry." Never one to lack determination or confidence, Jimmy realized his dream in the winter of 1949.

Martin tells the story on stage occasionally. Monroe's regular guitarist and lead singer, Mac Wiseman, was going home to Virginia for the Christmas holidays. Martin rode the bus, as legend has it, over the bleak, winter-bitten mountains and auditioned for Bill backstage at the "Opry." His audition tune was one of the old Monroe-Flatt standards, "The Old Crossroads." Jimmy got the job and stayed with Monroe, off and on, until 1954.

Martin matured during his years as a Blue Grass Boy, and Monroe was a good teacher. Most of Monroe's Decca work of the early 1950s featured Martin's strong rhythm guitar and lead voice, and most of this material is what we have come to know as classic Monroe: "Uncle Pen," "New Muleskinner Blues," "On and On," "When the Golden Leaves Begin to Fall," "Letter from my Darlin'," "A Voice from on High," "River of Death," "Rawhide," and "I'm Working on a Building." With the possible exception of Lester Flatt, Jimmy Martin was Bill Monroe's finest lead singer.

As great as he was with Monroe, Martin was allowed little chance to prove his merit as a solo lead singer. He had the talent and he knew it, and he was eager to prove it. But an opportunity did come in 1950 when he met a young high-tenor singer named Bobby Osborne.

Osborne was a dark-haired teen-ager from Kentucky who had already made his mark in bluegrass as a guitar player and singer with the Lonesome Pine Fiddlers in the late 1940s. Just as Martin was developing into one of the best lead singers around, so was Osborne becoming one of the great tenors, possibly the best bluegrass was ever to see. Jimmy and Bob met when the Blue Grass Boys played the old State Theater in the Lonesome Pine Fiddlers' hometown of Bluefield, West Virginia. They sang a few songs together and were impressed with the sound. It was in 1951 that Martin left Bill Monroe to join the Lonesome Pine Fiddlers. During Jimmy's stay in Bluefield the band was joined briefly by Bobby's thirteen-year-old brother, Sonny, who was becoming a good banjo player.

The singing of Jimmy Martin and Bobby Osborne was the epitome of the bluegrass duet. Jimmy's voice was hard and strong and had the mountain-inflected sound that was the trademark of bluegrass lead singing. Osborne had many of the same qualities in his tenor voice. He had the Monroe "bite," but his voice was higher and more natural than most bluegrass tenors. At Martin's encouragement, Osborne abandoned the guitar for the mandolin and they formed their own band. They received a contract from King Records, borrowed two of the Cline brothers from the Lonesome Pine Fiddlers, and made some definitive early bluegrass recordings in the summer of 1951: "Blue-Eyed Darlin'," "My Lonely Heart," "You'll Never Be the Same," and "She's Just a Cute Thing." This group was not one of the best bluegrass bands, but it might have been if it had stayed together. There was a war in Korea, and nineteen-year-old Bob Osborne was drafted into the marine corps. He was sent overseas in 1952 and Jimmy Martin returned to Bill Monroe, taking young Sonny Osborne with him as banjoist for the Blue Grass Boys.

Martin's stay with the Blue Grass Boys was an historic one. Some extremely powerful music was played and recorded between 1949 and Martin's final exit from the band in 1954. When Martin left Monroe, Bob Osborne had already returned from the war, and he and Sonny had reorganized as the Osborne Brothers. Sonny was an expert banjo picker by then, but their band wasn't doing well. They had nearly starved in the Knoxville area and had moved up to southern Ohio. That's where Jimmy found them and that's where they started their band, Jimmy Martin and the Osborne Brothers. They moved to Detroit and a contract with RCA Records.

Jimmy Martin and the Osborne Brothers constituted one of the finest and most short-lived bands in the history of bluegrass. By 1954 Martin was acknowledged as the best bluegrass singer around. Bob Osborne had the highest tenor in the business and had become a superb mandolin player. Sonny, still a teen-ager, was a fine banjo player and had mastered the difficult third part, or baritone, for the trio singing. It was the trios that really set this band apart from the rest. Their material was also noteworthy, being the first indication of the kind of thing Martin was trying to develop as the Jimmy Martin style.

The bluesy "20/20 Vision" is probably the best remembered of the 1954 RCA recordings, but it really wasn't much different from the songs the Lonesome Pine Fiddlers had recorded for the same label. Jimmy Martin's other RCA material was giving bluegrass a new look. He had discovered the novelty tune.

Martin's delving into the possibilities of bluegrass may have been a reaction to the really heavy stuff he had done with Monroe only a few years before, such mournful, poignant songs as "Letter from My Darlin'," "Memories of Mother and Dad," and "The Old Kentucky Shore." He was right in deciding that after four years with Monroe he was going to have to do something very different to establish his own identity as an artist.

Typical of the RCA Martin–Osborne tunes were "I Pulled a Boo Boo (I Think)" and "Save It! Save It!" They established the Martin "good 'n' country" pattern of bouncy, driving bluegrass with good singing and humorous, catchy lyrics. "Save It! Save It!" begins with someone (possibly Sonny) giving a wolf whistle and shouting, "Hey, baby!" and the wacky, suggestive song unfolds to a fast-paced bluegrass beat. It's an entertaining performance and a total departure from the intensely personal songs of Bill Monroe or the lonesome, mountain style of the Stanley Brothers. Jimmy was offering a welcome alternative.

If the songs were not to be taken seriously, the performances were. They were outstanding, with plenty of good banjo, mandolin, and fiddle. The fiddle and bass were provided by two of Monroe's finest sidemen, who were working as Nashville session musicians: fiddler Merle "Red" Taylor and bassist Howard "Cedric Rainwater" Watts.

Bob and Sonny Osborne left Detroit and Jimmy Martin in 1955. They moved to Wheeling to play with Charlie Bailey at the WWVA "Jamboree." Martin was quick to replace them with banjoist Sam Hutchins and mandolinist Earl Taylor, and the sound of the Sunny Mountain Boys remained essentially unchanged as Jimmy began establishing his reputation for a remarkable consistency of sound. Musicians would come and go over the years, but the driving Jimmy Martin "good 'n' country" sound would remain intact. Jimmy left RCA and moved to Decca, and the records with Earl Taylor playing mandolin and singing tenor are remembered as some of his best: "Rock Hearts," "I'll Drink No More Wine," and the omnipresent novelty zingers, "Hit Parade of Love," "Dog Bite Your Hide," "The Grand Ole Opry Song," and "Lost Ball in the High Weeds."

One noticeable thing about almost all major bluegrass bands is that each has enjoyed an artistic heyday, a period in which just the right musicians were assembled at the right place and time, resulting in a chemistry—an interaction of talents and personalities. In the case of Jimmy Martin and the Sunny Mountain Boys, these "right" musicians were in the form of a chubby mandolinist named Paul Williams and a banjo player named J. D. Crowe. Williams had helped the Lonesome Pine Fiddlers cut some of their best material in the early 1950s, and his thumpy, round-hole Gibson mandolin and strong tenor voice graced most of Martin's best Decca material of the late 1950s and early 1960s. Crowe was just a kid, so skinny that his Gibson Mastertone banjo, with it's heavy, chrome-plated look, threatened to pull him to the ground. But he could cut the straight Scruggs-style with the best of them, and he also had a distinctive style of his own, some of which could be heard to good advantage in the tune "Hold What You've Got" from their first Decca album. It was a style that combined a lot of the straight, conventional Scruggs technique with a syncopated bounce and off-beat blues licks that suited the buoyant, sassy Jimmy Martin style perfectly. The band clicked, and the tunes that Martin, Williams, and Crowe recorded together were some of the best-received and most-copied bluegrass of their day, such definitive Martin stuff as "Ocean of Diamonds," "You Don't Know My Mind," "Bear Tracks," "Hold What You've Got," "Sophronie," and others.

JIMMY MARTIN

The Jimmy Martin band of the late 1950s and early 1960s firmly established the sound that Jimmy called good 'n' country. It was the Jimmy Martin sound and no one else's, and Jimmy insisted that his musicians play no other style. Once a Jimmy Martin record is cut, that's exactly the way it will be played on stage—always. Whether the banjo player on the record was Sam Hutchins, J. D. Crowe, Paul Craft, Bill Emerson, or Vic Jordan, every banjo player in the Jimmy Martin band would play it exactly the same. This rigid, hard-nosed attitude has caused both Martin and his sidemen a lot of grief over the years. He allows little creativity, and the more creative musicians do not seem to want to stay with him very long. Insisting on the same sound is in many ways desirable, but it also has been one of the factors contributing to the endless turnover of Martin's personnel.

They have come and gone from the Jimmy Martin band; some have gone on to greater glory, while others became discouraged and abandoned music entirely. But good or mediocre, they all played the same music when they were with Martin: banjoists Sam Hutchins, Sonny Osborne, J. D. Crowe, Bill Emerson, Paul Craft, Vic Jordan, Chris Warner, Tim Spradlin, Al Munde and Kenny Ingram; mandolinists Earl Taylor, Paul Williams, Vernon Derrick, Billy Torbert, Doyle Lawson, Herschel Sizemore. None of them is with Jimmy Martin today. He is not known as being an easy man to work for. Other writers have noted that Jimmy Martin finds a great deal of humor in introducing his band members on stage with insults: Of Al Munde, Jimmy would say to the audience, "We wanted Tuesday, but we had to settle for Munde." Of bassist Gloria Belle, "She's not very good, but we let her sing with us 'cause we feel sorry for her." He's probably kidding us (and them) but it gets to be too much for some of the more thin-skinned musicians to take, and they leave Jimmy and move on. There's always someone there waiting to take his or her place.

Playing with a band like Jimmy Martin and the Sunny Mountain Boys was once something for young musicians to strive for. This is becoming less and less the case as bluegrass grows in popularity and other, better opportunities are at hand. Several of Jimmy's methods of handling people have become known, and the bad word has gotten around. It is just not that easy anymore to find a top-flight banjo player who is willing to put up with the Jimmy Martin personality.

Bill Emerson wrote a nice article on his former boss for *Bluegrass Unlimited* several years ago, sort of a "Jimmy Martin explained." He points

73

out that Jimmy's is an excitable, artistic temperament bolstered by a brassy ego. He seems never to have learned exactly how to handle his enormous musical gifts, or to accept graciously the fame and recognition that comes his way. He is a super-extrovert, and the same extrovert qualities that have made him such a winning showman have made him less than well loved in many quarters.

Sonny Osborne once said that if Jimmy Martin had just listened to some of the advice given him over the years, he would have been one of the biggest stars in the country. As it is, he hasn't gotten half the recognition his talent deserves. He has had records on the charts but no big hits. He has recorded so many of those silly novelty tunes—"Goin' Ape," "Guitar-Pickin' President," "I Can't Quit Cigarettes"—hoping that one might be catchy enough to catch on, but none of them has. He has guested on the "Opry," but he has never been invited to join the cast of that important show. If he had taken Sonny's advice, gone the Osborne Brothers' pop-country route, he probably would have gained top billing at the "Opry," as the Osborne Brothers have today. But he had stubbornly refused to compromise his sound. He is as loyal to his fans as they are to him, and he could never leave the thousands who have supported him over the years, the ones who loved him because he represented their faith in bluegrass. And because he has never broken the faith, he will probably never be the big star he hopes to be. Nashville just isn't ready for his kind of hard-line bluegrass—yet.

When the Nitty Gritty Dirt Band decided to make their "Circle" album, the name Jimmy Martin was on the list of legendary participating artists that included such immortals as Roy Acuff, Maybelle Carter, Earl Scruggs, Doc Watson, and Merle Travis. The album was the band's tribute to their musical roots, the young and old joining to complete the full circle of the development of country music. The album sold, and the most respected names of bluegrass and old-time music were put before a market that for the most part had never heard them perform. Jimmy Martin furnished some of his standard songs: "Sunny Side of the Mountain," "Walkin' Shoes," and "You Don't Know My mind." He was possibly the best thing on the album, and his performance certainly was a very forceful blow struck for bluegrass music.

As Martin ages, his bands can't quite match the quality of the old Crowe and Williams days. Or maybe they're the same and bluegrass has matured

74

around them. Once it could have been argued that Jimmy Martin had the best bluegrass band going. This may or may not be true today, but what remains certain is that Jimmy Martin, the tireless and unsinkable Sunny Mountain Boy, is still the king of the bluegrass lead singers.

7

Jim and Jesse

DEDICATION VERSUS
THE SURVIVAL INSTINCT

Brother or family acts have always been strong in country music. The old-style country music is family music, made at home to be enjoyed in the home. The lineage is easy to trace, from the Carters to J. E. and Wade Mainer, up through the best of the 1930s brother teams—the Monroes and Callahans, the Delmores and the Blue Sky Boys—through the 1940s with the Bailey Brothers and the Bailes Brothers, and into the 1950s with the Louvins and the Wilburn Brothers. The home-style harmonies of the brother duets have always been popular, and their acceptance into bluegrass was only logical.

The brother tradition is beautifully represented in the bluegrass world by the McReynolds Brothers, Jim and Jesse.

Again the story begins in the magic bluegrass circle in the mountains of central Appalachia. The town is Coeburn, Virginia, in the coal mining country very near the ancestral home of the Stanley Brothers. It was a musical family; the father and uncles had a string band that even made some records in the old days. Jim was the oldest, born in 1927, and he was given the rather patriotic name of James Monroe McReynolds. Less than two years later another boy was born, Jesse Lester McReynolds. As in most households in that area, the Monroe Brothers were listened to faithfully as the brothers became interested in music. Jim played mandolin and guitar, Jesse the mandolin and fiddle. By the mid-1940s they started their own band, the McReynolds Brothers and the Cumberland Mountain Boys, and they began playing on a jamboree-style Saturday night radio show in nearby Elizabethtown, Tennessee. It wasn't a bluegrass band; banjo players who played Scruggs-style weren't that common yet. They played the same type of music the other brother duets were playing. Jesse had settled on the mandolin as his primary instrument and sang lead; Jim, who was growing tall and handsome, concentrated on the guitar and sang tenor harmony.

From the beginning, Jim and Jesse's harmony has been special. In fact, they had then and still have today what is considered the most beautiful duet sound in bluegrass. Their career has been a checkerboard of changes, from old-time music to traditional western, from bluegrass to modern country, and back to bluegrass. But through it all they have kept their identity, their sound, their distinctive vocal blend.

Jim and Jesse sing so well it's hard to believe they are really from Coeburn, Virginia. Their blend is so remarkably pure and smooth, so unlike the hard-bitten sound of the Stanley Brothers, who were literally from the same time and place. To a point, the paths of the two bands crossed in several places. They both started their bands in the same area near Norton, Virginia, at about the same time. They both worked out of the "Suwannee River Jamboree" in Live Oak, Florida, in the late 1950s. They both recorded for Starday Records during their Florida years. But their styles couldn't be farther apart, and the differences are often pointed out to illustrate the variety of stylistic possibilities open to bluegrass artists.

A sound was developing in the late 1940s, and the McReynolds Brothers were very much aware of it. Earl Scruggs was at the "Opry," and Bill Monroe was forging his dynamic new style. The brothers were playing in Georgia in a band headed by Hoke Jenkins, the banjoist nephew of the great Snuffy Jenkins. Hoke played a rather rough three-finger style, and with the playing of Earl Scruggs and others all around him, Jesse wanted to try to duplicate the finger-picked banjo sound on his mandolin. Jenkins and Scruggs used the thumb and first two fingers in their style, but Jesse was determined to try to achieve the same effect using only a single straight pick. The result was a style called cross-picking. It was an amazing accomplishment, a brilliant and complicated technique far more difficult than the Scruggs-picked banjo.

In the early days of 1950 many young musicians were in the process of firmly establishing themselves in the Bill Monroe bluegrass camp. There was Don Reno, Mac Wiseman, Flatt and Scruggs, Bob Osborne, Jimmy Martin, the Stanley Brothers, and many others. Jim and Jesse McReynolds admired Monroe but seemed to see themselves as professional musicians first and bluegrass musicians second. The others had played with or would eventually end up with Monroe in Nashville. The McReynolds boys had no inclinations in that direction. In 1950, at a time when the others found themselves being drawn to Monroe, Jim and Jesse made a most unusual move—to Wichita, Kansas, far away from the bluegrass mountains of Virginia and Kentucky.

The time they spent in the Midwest had a great influence on the smooth sound for which they later became noted. They were playing a twice-daily radio program, doing the songs of the Sons of the Pioneers—a style characterized by sweet, smooth trios and slick arrangements. Their next move was to the southern Ohio area, where they made their first recordings, on the Kentucky label. These were primarily gospel trios, done with another singer named Larry Roll. The group was called the Virginia Trio, and their records were unusually fine examples of the artistry of Jim and Jesse, featuring the first examples of the penetrating, staccato complexity of the Jesse McReynolds cross-picked mandolin. The sound was smooth and gentle, with Jim's high, angelic tenor floating over the other parts on such numbers as "Sing, Sing, Sing," "I Like the Old-Time Way," and "God Put a Rainbow in the Clouds." Still, none of the cuts was bluegrass. There was no banjo, no fiddle. Just a guitar, three voices, and some mandolin playing that closely resembled a bluegrass banjo.

Actually, the McReynolds' career was, at best, unsettled through most of the early 1950s. Jesse was drafted, and the brothers were forced to abandon the act for two years, although Jim continued as a single. But the early 1950s were at least productive in that they made their recording debut as a full bluegrass band.

They had gotten a contract with Capitol Records, and Ken Nelson produced some excellent music with Jim and Jesse and some outstanding sidemen at the historic Tulane Hotel in Nashville. Hoke Jenkins recorded with them, as did legendary fiddler Tommy Jackson and Flatt and Scruggs' long-time mandolin player, Curly Sechler. Also at the sessions were fiddlers Tommy Vaden and Sonny James, who later became one of country music's biggest singing stars.

The Capitol songs were outstanding in many respects. Some of it was a bit rough (especially Jenkins' banjo work), but it was the full-blown Jim and Jesse sound. The duet singing featured Jim's beautiful, clear tenor blending with Jesse's polished, gentlemanly lead. The singing was superb, and the

The McReynolds Brothers flank one of their most famous Virginia Boys, banjoist Allen Shelton. (*Paul Gerry*)

"Once More." The Osborne Brothers and Johnny Dacus lean in for a close trio. Red Allen had just left the band. (*Paul Gerry*)

The Osborne Brothers today: Nashville's answer to modern bluegrass. Sonny, Bobby, and Dale Sledd abandoned their electric instruments for this performance. (*Karen Artis*)

Bill Monroe, still the supreme instrumentalist. Monroe's expression tells of the man's emotional intensity, a feeling that has been conveyed to his audiences for over forty years. (*Bill McIntire*)

The "Bluegrass Special," Bill Monroe's tour bus of the 1960s. The bus was road-worn when this photo was taken, having just been driven from Nashville to Los Angeles. (*Mark Ratkovic*)

Genial Jimmie Skinner has long been recognized as a friend to bluegrass as well as a performer in the Jimmie Rodgers tradition.

Mac Wiseman, "The Voice with a Heart," participated in some memorable sessions with Bill Monroe and Flatt and Scruggs before signing with Dot Records in the early 1950s and becoming a major star in his own right. Once a man of large proportions, Wiseman has recently slimmed down. (*Karen Artis*)

The inimitable Louvin Brothers, Ira and Charlie. The Louvins, popular in the country music world of the 1950s, were the last big guitar-mandolin act in "straight" country music, although the tradition thrives in bluegrass. Their influence on bluegrass was profound. Ira, shown frolicking in front of the microphone with his mandolin, died in an auto wreck in 1964. Charlie remains one of the top country singing stars. (*Paul Gerry*)

Kentucky balladeer Hylo Brown recorded some of the best bluegrass ever in the 1950s. (*Carl Fleischhauer*)

Almost as influential as the Louvin Brothers were Johnny and Jack. Johnny (Wright) and Jack (Anglin) were popular through the 1950s with a sound that was close to bluegrass, adding many songs to the repertoire of the bluegrass bands. Anglin was killed in an automobile accident in 1963. Wright still tours with his wife, country singer Kitty Wells. (*Paul Gerry*)

Giants of Washington blue-grass. Bill Clifton stands in the center in the light coat. Flanking him are the members of the "classic" Country Gentlemen group, Waller and Duffey (left and right of Clifton) and Gray and Adcock (kneeling). (*Paul Gerry*)

Earl Taylor, strong exponent of the Bill Monroe style of tenor singing and mandolin playing, was for many years a key man in the Washington-Baltimore area. (*Paul Gerry*)

Red Allen with a great band from his Washington years. Crew-cut Red holds the guitar, followed by legendary mandolinist Frank Wakefield, the late Robbie Robinson on banjo, and Tom Morgan on bass. (*Keith Russell*/Bluegrass Unlimited)

The irreverent clowns of bluegrass, the Country Gentlemen. Duffey and Adcock try to play behind their heads, followed by Charlie Waller and Ed Ferris. (*Paul Gerry*)

The original Greenbriar Boys: Eric Weissberg, John Herald, and Bob Yellin. City boys, the Greenbriars brought an enthusiasm to their music that drew many from the college and urban set into bluegrass. Weissberg, of *Deliverance* fame, was replaced by Ralph Rinzler, who has been a tremendous intellectual force in the bluegrass field. (*Paul Gerry*)

mandolin work was astounding. Jesse had become, as early as those Korean War years, the most technically advanced mandolin player bluegrass music would see for many years. Their fabulous harmony blend and brilliant instrumental work were heard to good advantage on such beautiful pieces as "Too Many Tears," "A Memory of You," "Just Wondering Why," and the songs that were to become Jim and Jesse standards, "Air Mail Special" and "Are You Missing Me?" Notable also were three fine cuts that featured the brothers singing in trio with the great Curly Sechler: "Are You Lost in Sin," "Look for Me (I'll Be There)," and Curly's Korean War ballad, "Purple Heart."

The records were well received, but the war in Korea and Jesse's involvement in it didn't do too much to help their career along. By the time the mandolinist returned and the band resumed operation, the rock 'n' roll boom was taking its toll on country music. Capitol was no longer interested in promoting bluegrass music, and cold economics caused a decided cooling between the brothers and their record company.

They played for a while at the WWVA "Jamboree" in Wheeling, one of the major programs of its kind that had served for many years as a minor league for the "Opry." The "Jamboree" brought the music of Jim and Jesse to a huge audience in the Northeast and Canada, and then the band moved to Live Oak, Florida, touring the deep South with the "Suwannee River Jamboree." The days of station-hopping were not over for many bands, even up through the late 1950s, but now the emphasis was on television instead of radio.

Times were still rough and things unsettled for the band when they moved to Valdosta, Georgia, but the move seemed to have a settling effect on them. They played at the "Lowndes County Jamboree" for the next few years, acquiring a band that would be remembered as their finest. The banjoist was a youngster named Bobby Thompson, whose style of picking would become as influential in the 1960s and 1970s as the styles of Scruggs and Reno had been in the years before. Their fiddler was a legend even then and was to become the best-known bluegrass fiddler in the world by the early 1970s. His name was Vassar Clements.

It was with Clements and Thompson that the McReynolds Brothers made their third trip into the recording studios. The sessions were held in Jacksonville, Florida (the same city that produced the classic Stanley Brothers records in those days of the late 1950s), and the music they made is still remembered as the classic Jim and Jesse: "Hard Hearted," "Changing the Words to My Love Song," "Let Me Whisper," and some unforgettable instrumentals. Two of the instrumentals were unusual in that neither featured the brilliant Jesse McReynolds' cross-picking style. One, "Border Ride," was a Spanish-sounding tune played in the conventional mandolin style. "Dixie Hoedown" had no mandolin at all: Jesse played a twin fiddle to Vassar Clements.

The most influential musician to come out of the Jim and Jesse band was Bobby Thompson. There has been a whole new school of bluegrass banjo players in recent years playing a style that has come to be known as chromatic. In much of straight Scruggs-style playing, the melody is only hinted at and is hidden among the shower of notes and rolled picking patterns. Complicated hornpipes and other fiddle-type tunes requiring an exact succession of individual notes and a precise melody line can't be adequately played in the style of Earl Scruggs, Ralph Stanley, or Don Reno. Thompson developed a style (at the suggestion of fiddler Benny Sims) in which his roll, or finger patterns, produced a straight chromatic scale. With a slight rearranging of the scales, complicated passages from the most complex fiddle tunes could be reproduced with complete accuracy.

There is some controversy as to who came up with the style first, Thompson or the great New England banjo player Bill Keith, who brought the style to country audiences while playing with Bill Monroe in the early 1960s. The style (or at least the technical basis for the style) had actually been around since the days of the classical banjo players at the turn of the century, but most likely Keith and Thompson arrived at the style independently of each other and of the nearly extinct school of classical masters. Bobby Thompson nearly vanished from the bluegrass scene after leaving Jim and Jesse, leaving Bill Keith the limelight. But Thompson has now come out of his premature retirement, and today he is one of the most sought-after sidemen in Nashville. If a five-string banjo is heard on any record from the Nashville music factory, chances are it's Bobby Thompson's. In any case, both Thompson and Keith are the most humble of men, and no feud exists between them.

The Jim and Jesse records featuring Thompson and Clements were recorded for and released on Don Pierce's Starday label, a Nashville-based operation—one of the few to continue circulating traditional country music after the rock takeover. The material was recorded in 1959, and that same year marked one of the more fortunate occurrences in the Jim and Jesse story. Like Flatt and Scruggs before them, they were adopted by the Martha White Flour Company.

JIM AND JESSE

Flatt and Scruggs had been working the television circuit under the Martha White banner through the mountain areas. Martha White had gotten Lester and Earl their spot on WSM radio and the "Grand Ole Opry." Now the same company sent Jim and Jesse and their Virginia Boys across the deep South: Georgia, Mississippi, Florida, and Alabama. They worked the TV shows sponsored by Martha White and generally followed the pattern established by the Flatt–Scruggs–Martha White relationship in the mid-1950s. It was the best thing that could have happened. They were soon playing on the "Grand Ole Opry" and hosting their own morning radio show from the WSM studios.

Their move to Nashville and their affiliation with one of the "Opry's" major sponsors opened many doors. The Martha White people brought their work to the attention of Columbia Records, Flatt and Scruggs' label, and they were signed to record for Columbia's Epic sublabel.

The Starday years may be remembered as their best, but the years at Epic were the most productive. Columbia was a big label, but Jim and Jesse were being given more artistic freedom than many groups, including Flatt and Scruggs. Columbia's Don Law must have felt that the McReynoldses had a more commercially acceptable sound than Lester and Earl's Foggy Mountain Boys. They were certainly the smoothest band in bluegrass, too smooth for the tastes of many hard-line bluegrass fans. Smoothness and professionalism had always been the hallmark of the Virginia Boys band, and their Epic group, which usually included fiddler Jim Buchanan and banjoist Allen Shelton, was the smoothest ever assembled.

The years at Epic produced a number of fine albums. The best remembered was one with the simple title "Bluegrass Special," and almost every song on it rapidly became standard in the bluegrass field: "Stoney Creek," "I Wish You Knew," and refreshing bluegrass versions of some of the popular traditional country songs they had heard as boys, "Don't Say Goodbye If You Love Me," "Somebody Loves You Darlin'," and the old-time "When It's Time for the Whippoorwill to Sing." Several consistently high-grade efforts followed, including the LPs "Bluegrass Classics," "The Old Country Church," "Kneel at the Cross," a tribute to country humor titled "Y'All Come," and a tasteful salute to rock star Chuck Berry called "Berry Pickin' in the Country."

Jim and Jesse McReynolds were not getting rich playing bluegrass music. They had recorded some best-ever bluegrass through the mid-1960s, but the word *bluegrass* was still taboo at most country radio stations. Nashville had been moderately successful in pulling itself out of the post-Elvis slump, but

81

it was at the cost of the more traditional aspects of the music. Bluegrass was still enjoying an acceptance in the colleges due to the folk music revival, but bands like Jim and Jesse and the Virginia Boys—touring, professional bands who depended on record sales, air-play, and public acceptance—were not getting the exposure they deserved and needed for survival. Being tagged "bluegrass" meant that no radio station in its right mind would play that record on the air, no matter how smooth and polished the performance or nontraditional the material.

Suddenly, in 1966, Jim and Jesse changed their style. They recorded a "straight" country tune called "Diesel on My Tail." It actually was a good song, but the inclusion of the electric guitar, pedal steel, drums, and pianos outraged the bluegrass camp. "Diesel on My Tail" was a major top-ten hit. Jim and Jesse had sold out.

Their overnight switch from bluegrass to country lost them the bluegrass following they had built up over so many years. They tried to make a go of it as a country band but were only moderately successful. They never came up with a follow-up to "Diesel" that would firmly establish their status as country stars. But the bluegrass festivals were now coming into their own, and most of the old-line bluegrass stars, Jim and Jesse included, saw them as the possible salvation of bluegrass music.

They were still on the musical fence. They carried a banjo player but featured him only on their show dates that were specifically "bluegrass." They had a pedal steel man who could double on the dobro if the occasion called for it. Then, in a move that raised false hopes as to their future as a bluegrass band, they rejoined Capitol. The hopes were dashed. Their Capitol singles were of the same bland pop-country quality as their later Epic output.

The festivals did save the Jim and Jesse bluegrass sound. They realized that a good living could be made and a top-notch band maintained through most of the year by the steady work offered by the summer bluegrass festivals. They weren't selling their country stuff at the festivals, and since much of the money made on the road involves the hawking of records, they produced a number of bluegrass LPs of their own production on the Prize and Old Dominion labels. Jim and Jesse still ride the musical fence, but they seem to be at peace with themselves. They have reached that proverbial happy medium that has made everyone a little more comfortable with the Jim and Jesse situation.

Through the lean years and the prosperous, through bluegrass and country, Jim and Jesse have never let their extremely high standards slip a single notch. Their beautiful vocal harmony remains today even purer and more direct than when they first started. They are an appealing duo, handsome and youthful-looking even though into their mid-forties, and their stage presentation is as incredibly precise as their best recordings. Jesse remains the top bluegrass mandolin virtuoso, and his cross-picking style has yet to be duplicated.

Jim and Jesse McReynolds are not without their detractors. Their music is too bland and sweet for some; too meticulously, predictably precise for others. But even a casual listen to Jesse's fabulous mandolin work on "Stoney Creek," "Dill Pickle Rag," and "El Cumbanchero," or the beautiful vocal blend and Jim's high, clear tenor on "When I Stop Dreaming" or "It's a Long, Long Way (to the Top of the World)" will reveal the tremendous gifts these two gentlemen from Virginia have brought to bluegrass.

8

The Osborne Brothers

CONTROVERSY AND ROCKY TOP, TENNESSEE

The mid-1950s were times of severe changes for most country musicians. The postwar country music boom had come to an abrupt halt. Hank Williams was dead and the rumblings from the direction of Memphis turned into a major earthquake when Sun Records executive Sam Phillips began releasing the tunes of young men who had been influenced by the sounds of rhythm and blues, as well as white gospel and hillbilly music. Johnny Cash was the most "country" of the lineup, which included Carl Perkins, Jerry Lee Lewis, and Elvis Presley. Someone coined the term *rock 'n' roll*, and the kings and queens of Nashville—the Roy Acuffs and the Kitty Wellses—soon learned that the damage was severe. Lewis recorded Hank Williams' "You Win Again," and Presley did Bill Monroe's "Blue Moon of Kentucky," but the beat was different, the instruments were different, the whole sound was not the one that Nashville had been pushing. Tastes were changed almost overnight as Presley replaced Ernest Tubb on truckstop jukeboxes all over the country. Nashville was forced into change, and if bluegrass had seemed out of place in the ever-commercializing trends of the "music city," then it was galaxies away from the new sound of rockabilly.

In the midst of the confusion, MGM Records auditioned and recorded a band headed by two brothers from Kentucky. They were a bluegrass band, and the emergence of the band called the Osborne Brothers was to have an effect on bluegrass music that was as profound as the one Elvis had on Nashville. And to some, almost as devastating.

The Osborne Brothers first saw the light of day in eastern Kentucky's coal mining country at a little town called Hyden. In 1969 it was the scene of a major mining disaster, the first time Hyden ever made the national headlines. Bob Osborne was born there in 1931, Sonny Osborne in 1937.

The story of the Osborne family and others like them is almost a cliché in bluegrass lore. They were the Depression-born of the mountains, and times were harder in central Appalachia than almost anywhere. Thousands of families moved north to places like Detroit, Baltimore, Cleveland, and Columbus, where they found good jobs in the factories and refineries and tried to make new and better lives for themselves and their families. They didn't miss the hard times, but the mystique of the mountains had made its impression on the minds and memories of the Kentucky and West Virginia immigrants. Just as the English and Scotch-Irish brought their culture and music to the New World, people like the Osbornes brought the music and culture of the mountains to the industrial North. The Blue Ridge and the Great Smokies were the initial breeding grounds of bluegrass, but the rolling hills and smoky cities of the central Midwest became the primary places of its growth and development in the 1950s.

Robert Osborne, Sr., arrived with his family in Dayton, Ohio, shortly after World War II and found employment at the National Cash Register plant there. The elder Osborne was musical, and his love for country music was passed on to his children. Bobby, the oldest, was the first to take an active interest in music. He was an Ernest Tubb fan, and his father bought him an electric guitar, which the youth played while singing Tubb's hits of the day. In the mid-1940s he was infected by the fatal virus: He heard the new sound from WSM and the "Grand Ole Opry," the music of Bill Monroe and his Blue Grass Boys. Flatt and Scruggs were with Monroe then, and Bobby began teaching himself to play the guitar like Lester Flatt and sing like Bill Monroe.

There was hardly ever a time when Bobby Osborne wasn't planning a career in music. He was only sixteen when he began playing in groups around Middletown, Ohio. He had his own band by 1949, a group that was a combination of electric-country and bluegrass, more or less in the style of country singer Jimmie Skinner. They took their music to station WPFB in Middletown, where Bob met a man who was to have a profound influence on his musical tastes, banjoist Larry Richardson.

Richardson was from the town of Mt. Airy, North Carolina, in an area that had always been one of the richest in traditional music. He was an outstanding tenor lead singer as well as one of the better Scruggs-style banjo pickers in those early days. If Osborne had been reluctant to take the plunge into bluegrass, the strong musical personality of Larry Richardson was more than enough to push him over the edge.

Bobby's voice had changed by the summer of 1949, but it was still a high, natural tenor, capable of reaching above high A with the ease of an operatic tenor. Both Larry and Bob had voices that could match or surpass Monroe's in range, and WPFB was unaware that it had one of the great early bluegrass duets on its meager payroll. They were together on the station only a month when an argument with the management caused Richardson to quit. Osborne soon followed.

Bobby Osborne quit high school to follow Richardson on a barnstorming tour of Ohio, trying to find a radio station interested in their music. None seemed to recognize their talent. South seemed the logical direction to go, and they found themselves in the mountain town of Bluefield, West Virginia. The station was WHIS and the band they played with was one headed by Rex and Eleanor Parker, but there was another band at the station they found a little more to their liking; the Lonesome Pine Fiddlers.

The Lonesome Pine Fiddlers had been around for a decade before Osborne and Richardson joined them. It consisted of various members of the Cline family, represented that autumn of 1949 by bassist-leader Ezra Cline. They were not a bluegrass band when Bob and Larry came aboard, but they were very soon to become one. By the early months of 1950 they had reached the recording studio, cutting four sides for the small Cozy label, making the Lonesome Pine Fiddlers one of the first bands to record what could be accurately described as "classic" bluegrass. The songs and performances are not remembered as being exceptional, but they were good, solid bluegrass: "Lonesome, Sad, and So Blue," "Will I Meet My Mother in Heaven?" "Don't Forget Me," and the song Flatt and Scruggs made into a standard on the Mercury label, Osborne and Richardson's own "Pain in My Heart."

Osborne's young brother, Sonny, was only twelve when the Cozy material was recorded. He had yet to see his first banjo picker when he went to Bluefield to visit Bob at WHIS. His interest in music in general and the banjo in particular was sharpened considerably after seeing Richardson in action. He went back to Ohio and talked his father into buying him a banjo. Records by Earl Scruggs and Ralph Stanley were memorized between farm chores, sports, and schoolwork, and Sonny's determination to become a musician became even greater than Bob's.

THE OSBORNE BROTHERS

It was inevitable that the Bill Monroe band would come through Bluefield. Bobby had seen them before, back when Monroe had Flatt and Scruggs with him, but now Monroe had another guitar man, a kid not much older than Bob named Jimmy Martin. The Blue Grass Boys played the old State Theater in Bluefield, and Martin and Osborne met, sang together backstage, and became friends. Jimmy's voice had become full and confident during the year or so he had been touring with Bill, gaining him the same kind of reputation as a lead singer that Bob had as a tenor, and their voices were as well matched as any in the business.

Larry Richardson has always been an enigma in bluegrass lore. He was in and out of great bands, made too few recordings. Everything he recorded could easily fit into the "classic" category of sought-after collector's items. He would occasionally surface and do something spectacular, then sink back into obscurity. He had been with the Lonesome Pine Fiddlers for only a year, helping to forever establish that band's identity as a bluegrass group, when he left Bluefield. Again Bob Osborne followed, though both rejoined the group very shortly thereafter. Larry stayed the second time through most of the spring of 1951 but left again, this time to play at the very important early bluegrass radio station, Bristol's WCYB. News reached the Fiddlers that Jimmy Martin was leaving Bill Monroe, and Martin was called to West Virginia as the Lonesome Pine Fiddlers' lead singer. Martin was one of the best rhythm guitarists in the business, and the decision was made to put Bob Osborne on the mandolin. An old Gibson mandolin was readily purchased, and Bob was on his way to establish himself as a tenor-singing mandolin player in the tradition of Bill Monroe.

Meanwhile young Sonny Osborne had been doing his banjo homework in Ohio. He spent much of his summer vacation in 1951 in West Virginia playing with Bob and Jimmy and the Lonesome Pine Fiddlers. When he returned home to continue school, Osborne and Martin quit the Fiddlers to start their own band.

Martin and Osborne had become one of the best bluegrass duets when they formed their own band in 1951. An audition with King Records proved to be successful, and they made some memorable recordings for King late that same summer. Two of the members of their band were brothers, members of the talented Cline family, Charlie and Curly Ray.

The Cline brothers were nephews of the Lonesome Pine Fiddlers' leader, Ezra Cline. Both were fine musicians and both contributed heavily to the development of early bluegrass sound through their work with the Fiddlers, Martin and Osborne, and other important groups. Charlie is best

87

remembered as Bill Monroe's star sideman through most of the 1950s. He was featured mainly as a fiddler and baritone singer with the Blue Grass Boys, and his work may be heard on many of the superb Bill Monroe Decca recordings of those early years. He was also featured on guitar, bass, banjo, and even mandolin during his years with Monroe at the "Opry." Curly Ray Cline was the instrumental backbone of the Lonesome Pine Fiddlers from the band's earliest days to their final breakup in the mid-1960s. His fiddle style is the perfect fusion of the old-time styles and the contemporary bluegrass style. Curly Ray joined Ralph Stanley in 1966 and continues to make memorable music as a vital part of the Stanley sound.

The sound achieved on those King recordings of 1951 was fine, old-style bluegrass. Bob was not yet a mandolin player and his mandolin work was too weak to warrant taking leads, but his sky-high tenor soared on the four numbers. Martin offered ample proof that he was becoming the bluegrass singer's singer on their material: "You'll Never Be the Same," "Blue-Eyed Darlin'," "My Lonely Heart," and "She's Just a Cute Thing." Charlie Cline contributed an adequate banjo, but one of the real highlights of the session was Curly Ray's fiddling, some of the best early bluegrass fiddling ever recorded.

There is no way to tell how long Osborne and Martin would have stayed together or how far they might have gone. They were a fantastic duet and they had a good band to back them up. But like so many others who had spent their early teens tuning in Bill Monroe and his great mid-1940s band on the "Grand Ole Opry," Bob Osborne was called into the service to fight in Korea.

Martin and Osborne had moved to WCYB in the Tennessee–Virginia border town of Bristol. The Stanley Brothers were there, recently reorganized after Carter's tour of duty with the Bill Monroe band, and Bobby worked with them as a mandolinist for a few weeks before reporting for induction at the marine corps recruiting center. His year as a front-line Marine in Korea was marked by a near-tragedy: At Panmunjom six fragments from an exploding mortar shell hit the twenty-year-old Kentuckian. Four of the pieces went into the side of his head, lodging in his temple. His steel helmet prevented the metal from doing much damage, and he was soon back in action.

He was missed at home. His sister Louise wrote a song about him titled "A Brother in Korea," which the Osbornes later recorded. Charlie and Curly Ray's sister, Patsy Cline (not related to the late country singer of the same name), wrote "My Brown-Eyed Darlin'" for Bob, whom she later married. It became one of the best-remembered songs of the Lonesome Pine Fiddlers.

Sonny had become a fair Scruggs-style banjo player by the time Bob was drafted. When Martin returned to Bill Monroe's band in 1952, he took the young Osborne with him. Charlie Cline was Monroe's fiddler, and Sonny Osborne, just fourteen years old, instantly rose from the obscurity of the southern Ohio farm country to become Bill Monroe's banjo player at the "Grand Ole Opry."

Sonny Osborne was unprepared for the stardom of Nashville. He was almost totally inexperienced and just wasn't of the same caliber as the men who had come before him, men like Earl Scruggs, Don Reno, and Rudy Lyle. He would eventually become one of the greats, but he was hardly ready for that first recording session, held just days after joining the Monroe group.

Admittedly, the recordings they made in those July days of 1952 were not noted for their great banjo playing. Sonny was not familiar with their material, not familiar with the musicians, and was scared to death of the bigger-than-life figure of Bill Monroe.

Still, it was a good band. With Martin, Cline, and bassist Ernie Newton, the Blue Grass Boys had a unity and tightness of sound that some bands never achieve, and Sonny displayed a sense of taste and timing that held the band's sound together. The recordings were all good, but the best remembered of those sessions were the numbers on which the banjo wasn't featured: "In the Pines," "Walking in Jerusalem Just Like John," "Memories of Mother and Dad," and "Little Girl and the Dreadful Snake." A shaky fourteen-year-old played adequate banjo breaks in "My Dying Bed," "Don't Put Off 'Til Tomorrow," and "Pike County Breakdown." Sonny always has been unnecessarily critical of his work on those records. He was no Earl Scruggs, to be sure, but his work with Monroe marked the professional recording debut of one of the most important recording artists in the bluegrass field.

Sonny left Monroe and the Blue Grass Boys at the end of that summer. When he returned home, in the best local-boy-makes-good tradition, Sonny found that he was somewhat of a celebrity. He teamed up with two excellent local musicians, Enos Johnson and Carlos Brock, to do some "cover" records for the Gateway label. The "covers" were recordings that were copies of the hits of other bluegrass artists, especially Flatt and Scruggs and

BLUEGRASS

Bill Monroe: "Rose of Old Kentucky," "We'll Meet Again, Sweetheart," and others. There was nothing original about the music, but there was one cut on which Sonny showed a young imagination at work, a tune called "Sunny Mountain Chimes." This tune, which was probably the biggest seller ever for the small Gateway label, established Sonny, still only fourteen years old, as a major bluegrass banjo player and quickly became one of the standard bluegrass banjo instrumentals.

Sonny had gotten the bug. He quit high school and by the summer of 1953 was back on the road with Bill Monroe and Jimmy Martin. But brother Bob had finished his time with the marines and was home. Sonny left Monroe for the last time and the Osborne Brothers were back in business.

Sonny had advanced almost unbelievably on the banjo in the two years that Bob had been away. Equally amazing was the way in which Bob had become expert on the mandolin in the foxholes of Korea. They were both ready to conquer the world. The opportunity to record came very shortly after Bob's return to civilian life. They were back in the Gateway studio doing more Flatt–Scruggs–Monroe copies to be sold as one of those record "package" bargains that are still common on the smaller radio stations. The music was outstandingly straight bluegrass, and Bobby all but out-Monroed Monroe with his vocals on "Muleskinner Blues" and "When the Golden Leaves Begin to Fall," while instrumentally these records proved that both Sonny and Bobby had matured into two of the top players of their day.

Their Gateway recordings of "Jesse James," "Silver Rainbow," "Walking Cane," and others showed Bobby Osborne to be one of the supreme mandolin stylists. His was a brittle, penetrating style that condensed more notes into a break than anyone had ever played before. His flashy, jazzy, multi-noted style was years ahead of its time, laying the groundwork for much of the "hot" progressive mandolin playing of the 1960s and 1970s.

The Osbornes took their music to Knoxville. The Tennessee town had for many years been a country music center, and many of the artists worked under the auspices of businessman Cas Walker at stations WROL and WNOX. Knoxville had been good to many country musicians, but Bob and Sonny starved out. They couldn't find enough work to keep them and their musicians fed, so they packed it up and moved back to Dayton. As luck would have it, Jimmy Martin had left Monroe by 1954 and was heading a band in their part of the country. The three united in what was probably the most inevitable act in the history of bluegrass.

THE OSBORNE BROTHERS

The reunion of Jimmy Martin and the Osborne Brothers in the summer of 1954 marked the joining of three immense talents, young men just beginning to realize their full potential as singers and instrumentalists. Their apprenticeship was complete, their enthusiasm high. Their joining marked the end of the long learning period and the beginning of a memorable musical association, as well as the beginning of two highly successful careers in bluegrass music. They acquired a regular radio spot in Detroit, an area rich in Kentucky and Virginia migration culture. A contract with RCA resulted in some of the strongest bluegrass ever recorded, including the Jimmy Martin classic, "20/20 Vision."

The great band folded almost as quickly as it had developed. By the summer of 1955 Bob and Sonny had moved to Wheeling to play with Charlie Bailey at the WWVA "Jamboree." Charlie Bailey had been half of the famous Bailey Brothers team from the Knoxville area. Sonny and Bob worked as Charlie's sidemen for a while, recording a few gospel cuts for one of the WWVA souvenir record packages. The association with Bailey didn't work out, and a few months later they were back in Dayton.

It might be said that the Osborne Brothers' story didn't start until they returned home in 1955. They decided that they would never be content to be sidemen. They knew they had something a little bit special, something that would set them apart if they could only find the right format. They bitterly took on menial daytime work while playing the dives and honky-tonks around their hometown.

The bars in southern Ohio were not nice places to work. Knifings were common, shootings almost nightly occurrences. The stage was often built high off the floor so the musicians would be less likely to get in the way of flying beer bottles, and the tight-fisted bar owners were willing to pay only a few dollars per man. Most groups couldn't afford to carry more than three musicians, severely altering the full bluegrass sound. The bare minimum was guitar, banjo, and mandolin; a fourth man constituted an economic unreality.

The thick cigarette smoke and smell of sweat and stale beer drained much of the purity from the music, and bands were forced to play their music faster and louder in order to be heard over the raucous, rowdy crowd. Most bands were compelled to fill as many audience requests as possible, which usually meant nonbluegrass dance tunes of a type unsuited to the style. While Flatt and Scruggs and the Stanley Brothers were playing the little mountain schoolhouses and movie theaters, bands like the Osborne

Brothers were driving cabs all day and playing in the grimy southern Ohio gin mills at night. They weren't the only ones. Also playing the same circuit was another Kentuckian, Harley "Red" Allen. The Osborne Brothers and Red Allen would get together after hours and sing, and the result was terrific.

Red had more power and range to his voice than anyone, and his trios with the Osborne Brothers were some of the best ever. In those days of the mid-1950s, when rock was knocking all the pins from under the country music industry, the little group from southern Ohio auditioned for and won a contract with MGM Records. Within a very short time the Osbornes were back at the WWVA "Jamboree," stars in their own right.

The bluegrass world has never really recovered from the band that walked on stage in Wheeling in 1956. They had a trio—a beautiful, smooth, forceful, sensational trio. Almost overnight the Osbornes and Red Allen shifted the bluegrass vocal emphasis from the duet to the trio. And aside from that, Bobby Osborne had a song, a vocal tour de force called "Ruby."

"Ruby" was probably the number that won them the MGM contract. It was a traditional-sounding number, learned from an old record by a singer named Cousin Emmy. Bobby sang it so high and with such power that listeners could scarcely believe they were hearing it. The sustained high notes on the chorus were something few bluegrass tenors could duplicate and established Bobby as the reigning high singer in bluegrass. The song drove along with two banjos instead of one, with Bob singing solo all the way through until the end. Then he was joined on a smooth, slow chorus ending, one of the Osbornes' many innovations in the bluegrass field. "Ruby" tore the roof off the Wheeling "Jamboree" hall and sold a lot of records for MGM.

The Osborne Brothers tried to duplicate the success they had with "Ruby" with such similar numbers as "Ho, Honey, Ho" and "Della Mae," but neither made the grade. Their music through the mid-1950s was a combination of traditional bluegrass, like Charlie Monroe's "Down in the Willow Garden" and Red's "Teardrops in My Eyes," and the more modern-sounding things that were probably holdovers from their days in the honky-tonks of Dayton and Middletown. They were still searching for a distinctive sound that might give them an edge over the country acts that were floundering against the new sounds of rock. Aggressive drums were used on some of their records, tunes like "Love Pains" and "If You Don't, Somebody Else Will." They finally found the sound that was to be the Osborne

Brothers' trademark. It was a trite country weeper learned from a Wheeling singer named Dusty Owens called "Once More."

Before "Once More," the brothers had stayed within the traditional limits of bluegrass harmony. The lead singer sang the song in a middle register, joined on the chorus by a tenor and a baritone. On "Once More" they changed the parts. Bobby sang the lead, but way up high in his high, tenor range. Sonny sang his regular baritone, while Red, instead of singing lead, sang a tenor harmony an octave lower. So the high voice sang the melody instead of the harmony, and the arrangement spotlighted the beautiful, incredibly high voice of Bob Osborne. The result was a smoothness of harmony, a polished sound that literally rewrote the book on bluegrass singing. There were other songs, too: "(Is This) My Destiny," "It Hurts to Know," and "Lost Highway," but "Once More" was the greatest. It was possibly the most revolutionary performance in the history of bluegrass.

Red Allen stayed with the Osbornes through 1958. There was trouble within the band, probably over general approach. The differences in their musical opinions can best be illustrated by the kinds of music Allen and the Osbornes went on to play: The Osbornes have always been at the front of the progressive, innovative school of bluegrass; Red Allen became a champion of the strict traditionalists. Red was gone, but the Osbornes had found their style, and while Red was instrumental in its formulation, he wasn't needed for its execution. Bobby had proved himself as a lead singer and they were never again to depend on the talents of a forceful guitarist-lead singer.

Fiddler Johnny Dacus replaced Allen on guitar, and the role of their guitarists was firmly established: They would be hired to strum a bland rhythm and sing the subtle, low harmony in the Bobby-dominated trios. So it has been with every guitarist they have had since: Jimmy Brown, Benny Birchfield, Gordon Cash, Ronnie Reno, and Dale Sledd.

The innovations of Bob and Sonny Osborne were scorned by traditionalists from the first. The heavy drums on some of the Osborne–Allen records raised many eyebrows, as did the inclusion of electric guitars and steel guitars on some of their later MGM work, notably the beautiful "Fair and Tender Ladies," with Benny Birchfield. They were reaching for a hit and their sound became accordingly commercial. Rock, of course, made the idea of any country or bluegrass song becoming a hit a little less than likely, but the Osbornes were in there trying. Only one number they recorded was an out-and-out attempt at rock, but the product hardly warranted the effort. It was a full electric thing called "There's a Woman Behind Every Man," and it didn't work.

Folk music was the partial salvation of a lot of traditional country music, and the Osborne Brothers paved the way to the college campus with their important engagement at Antioch College, Ohio, in 1959. It established a precedent, and thereafter no college folk festival was complete without at least one bluegrass-style band. Much to the Osbornes' surprise, the young collegians went more for their traditional Monroe-style bluegrass than the rock and country numbers they presented.

Things moved faster for Bob and Sonny as the 1950s became the 1960s. Unhappy about the deal they were getting from Wheeling as well as MGM, they made contacts with Nashville (Doyle Wilburn of the Wilburn Brothers, to be exact) and arranged a contract with Decca Records, which led to an end of the rainbow—that ever-important spot on the "Grand Ole Opry." Decca did give them a better deal, allowing them as much artistic freedom as they wanted. The result was a string of fine, modern bluegrass LPs, outstanding in their almost painful-beautiful trios, songs like "A Pathway of Teardrops," "Kentucky," and "This Heart of Mine (Can Never Say Goodbye)." One LP bore the title "Voices in Bluegrass," and that's what it was, combined with some of their distinctive, flashy instrumental work. Another, titled "Up This Hill and Down," provided them with their first hit on the country charts and heralded the major changes about to take place. The addition of piano did not go unnoticed by the more tradition-oriented. Another LP was released called "Modern Sounds of Bluegrass Music," which featured the entire Nashville menagerie of electric guitars, a move that alienated many of the loyalists. Not the least offensive thing about "Modern Sounds" to hard-core fans was a set of liner notes by Teddy Wilburn (the other Wilburn brother) telling everyone how bad acoustic bluegrass was going to sound after they'd heard this record.

Decca began producing major hits for the Osborne Brothers, one of the biggest of which dealt with a fictional Tennessee mountain community called "Rocky Top." It was a fast, pounding song, totally bluegrass in feeling, with a lot of good banjo and mandolin, and a storyline about the mountain boy who wishes he was back on the mountain, away from smog and telephone bills. It was light-hearted, fun, and it sold. Still, because the subject matter wasn't the heaviest and there was a pedal steel guitar in the background, most dour-faced sticklers didn't care for it and failed to acknowledge the fact that a bluegrass record was actually getting an enormous amount of air-play on the country stations.

Other hits followed, much after the "Rocky Top" formula: "Listening to the Rain," "Georgia Piney Woods," "Tennessee Hound Dog." But by the time the others had come out, the Osbornes had taken the final plunge: In 1969 they electrically amplified their banjo and mandolin. The uproar from the ranks of tradition was deafening.

The Osborne Brothers came into the 1970s full speed ahead. They were trying to make it as a stage act and were doing a hell of a job. Always fat, (to be blunt), they both slimmed down to acceptably attractive weights; Bobby sprouted stylish sideburns while Sonny became known for his pointed chin whiskers. They were at the center of the bluegrass storm and were basking in the glory. And the instruments? After electronic bugs were worked out, their basic sound remained intact. The banjo sounded like a banjo and the mandolin sounded like a mandolin, only both were a lot louder and more impressive-sounding than the standard, nonelectric instruments. Looking back, the whole thing seems a little foolish, all the uproar over a length of insulated wire. The modern country audiences had to see a piece of wire coming out of the back of an instrument before they could enjoy the music. The same piece of wire sent traditionalists into a rage of protests. It was a reaction to a visual stimulus; the music was the same.

The purists have scratched the name Osborne off their lists forever. Many excluded them from discussions of the great bluegrass artists because they felt that the Osbornes sold out to the Nashville sound. To a certain extent, they have. But they are young musicians, and they are in the position of having to make a living as professional entertainers. If they hadn't updated their sound, they would probably still be driving cabs back in Dayton instead of being stars of the "Grand Ole Opry." As young, vital stars of the Nashville scene, they are bringing bluegrass to audiences that might otherwise never have been exposed to it. Osborne Brothers' records get the air-play, not Bill Monroe's records, and it's that kind of exposure that insures national acceptance.

Bobby and Sonny Osborne have done well. They are constantly voted among the top vocal groups in country music. Their records appear on the charts with regularity. It can hardly matter to them that the ranks of die-hard traditionalists don't care for their sound. They have been providing bluegrass with a much-needed thrust for almost twenty years, bringing about changes that even the most fanatic loyalist must see as necessary in the evolution of a music style that was founded on change. They have, on occasion, overdone it. But if bluegrass music is alive and well in the 1970s, it is due in no small part to the two courageous young men from Hyden, Kentucky.

9

Twenty-Five Years
of Hungry Bluegrass

YOU CAN PICK IT,
BUT YOU CAN'T EAT IT

Bill Monroe is not a hard man to spot at a bluegrass festival. He stands out, a lordly prince strolling among his subjects. He is a tall man, well over six feet, and his ever-present wide-brimmed Stetson is spotlessly white. He carries his sixty-plus years with pride and grace and holds that mandolin—that battered old Gibson that has had so much great music poured from its sound holes—like a royal scepter. Thick, curly gray hair bulges from under the hat, long and brushed back, silvery over the collar of a tailor-made, navy-blue pinstriped suit. A scarlet rose glares from the lapel as his handmade leather cowboy boots dodge the stumps and stones on the way to the stage.

His presence turns more than a few heads, and the whispers buzz through the audience like a swarm of bees. A heavy, farmish woman elbows her sunburnt husband, "Go up and ask him to play 'Uncle Pen,'" she hisses girlishly in his ear.

"Naw, Bill don't take requests."

"What do you mean, he don't take requests? Didn't he sing 'Walk Softly on My Heart' for us last night?"

"Yeah, but that's because we yelled it up from the audience. And besides, he was probably gonna sing it anyway."

"Well," she harumphs, "he don't scare me. I'll go up and ask him myself."

The awestricken farmer's wife raises herself from her folding lawn chair, but a little girl has already stopped Bill, clutching an autograph book and a ball-point pen. Bill kneels and gives her a broad, fatherly smile, asking the girl's name. She says it's Mary, a name Monroe uses frequently in his songs.

"Mary, I'm gonna show you something I learned when I was just about your age, and I'll bet you can't tell me how I do it."

The girl is mystified as Bill takes a circle of string from his coat pocket and twines it around and through his fingers to form a "Jacob's ladder," then makes it magically disappear again. The little girl is openmouthed as Bill smiles even more broadly and signs her book.

He straightens up, resumes his placid reserve, and walks down the steep hill toward the stage, where in a few moments he will be proving again, for possibly the millionth time, that he is indeed *the* great man of bluegrass.

Bill Monroe looks good. His bearing is at the same time calmly regal and arrogant. He has aged since the years he first set foot on the stage of the "Grand Ole Opry" but he has aged gracefully with the knowledge that he is the father of a unique and valid music style unlike any other and that there are literally thousands all over the world who worship his name.

Bluegrass music is doing well. The stars are all gaining weight and none of the younger musicians has that Depression-starved Appalachian look. Young mandolinist Jimmy Gaudreau looks like a junior executive, Sam Bush looks like a hip-but-clean-cut high school senior. Even the older stars today have a chubby, contented look—a far cry from the sunken-eyed bands that used to appear on stage in rumpled white dress shirts and limp, clip-on string ties.

The days of real hunger are still remembered. It hasn't been that long since the major names in the business were driving all night with the bass fiddle tied with rope to the top of a beat-up car for a few hundred dollars. They are dim memories, and the artists look on them with a little distaste. But the older fans recall the days with a touch of sadness, something about the music having more of a bite to it in the old days. Sure, it had a bite, but it was born probably out of desperation and frustration more than anything else. Life was rough and the musicians were frantically trying to make it. They had to keep the edge on it.

The musicians all ride big buses now, converted Greyhounds with built-in bunks and washrooms, almost like traveling hotels. The tour coaches of the bluegrass stars still haven't reached the elegance of the really posh rigs the Nashville stars drive around in—with card rooms and color TVs—but it certainly beats riding six hundred miles in the backseat of a 1957 Pontiac with three or four other people like they used to do.

BLUEGRASS

Back then it was a labor of love and subsequent sacrifice, and the love affair was often stretched to its limits. The long mountain drives were grueling, and it's a wonder so many survived intact. They were all in their share of car wrecks, and Earl Scruggs' near-fatal accident in 1955 caused him to take up flying; his doctor advised him that it would be safer and less taxing physically. With other groups, it was alcohol that provided relief from the boredom between low-paying schoolhouse and theater jobs. Worse yet were the hillbilly roadhouses and honky-tonks, which usually meant twice the work at half the pay while fighting off (or becoming) drunks. Malnutrition among traveling musicians was not uncommon then, and the quantities of alcohol on empty stomachs left several with physical problems as well as emotional ones. It's little wonder that some of the older bluegrass stars look fifteen years older than they really are.

Not everyone stayed with it. The more realistic-minded changed their brand of music to something that showed more possibilities of financial gain. Fiddlers Benny Martin and Gordon Terry both became pop-country singers. Chubby Wise, Bobby Hicks, Bobby Thompson, Mack Magaha and dozens of others found it more to their creditors' benefit to make a go of it as country and western sidemen. Others gave up entirely, relying on the steady income of the mines and mills, the machine shops and the service stations. Some, frankly, hit the skids and became drunks, while others underwent religious conversions and took up preaching, either limiting their playing to church functions or foregoing music entirely.

The lucky ones have been able to survive without making serious compromises in their music or taking severe physical and emotional beatings in the process.

A few years ago I had to make a long, cross-country drive to the West Coast. Being a devout bluegrass fan, I kept my radio dial in constant motion, trying to find that fabled station that deigned to play one or two bluegrass tunes an hour. Sure enough, somewhere in southern Ohio near the Kentucky state line, I heard the rippling ring of a five-string banjo hammering out the old hymn "I'll Fly Away." The station faded before I could find out who was doing the playing, but another spin of the dial produced yet another bluegrass band, obviously live and not very good, singing another hymn, "Power in the Blood." I drove behind a mountain and the signal faded. I tried a third station and almost ran off the road as yet another bluegrass band was found, this time a female trio singing "Leaning on the Everlasting Arms."

Then it dawned on me. The broadcasts were from tiny stations that set their microphones up in the local storefront Pentecostal and Holiness tabernacles every Sunday for a few hours of old-time foot-stomping, speak-in-tongues religion. I suddenly realized that here was one reason why some of the bluegrass musicians have given up the road work and taken their music to church. First, since the fundamentalist sects have services all week, the work is steady and assured. Second, being associated with a church is honest, clean, and respectable. Third, church people (being good and generous Christians) are less hostile to the idea of parting with a buck if it's in the name of the church.

Mercenary? Perhaps. Some, of course, have made the switch out of sincere faith. Others realize that the world's healthiest people are the ones who eat three times a day.

A lot of the better bands have found refuge in the church while the storms of change tossed the others around. Probably the best known is Carl Story's band. If there is a Mr. Bluegrass Gospel, Story undoubtedly wears the title, and his longevity at the top of the bluegrass field is a sterling lesson in survival. He had what was perhaps the first bluegrass-style band in the Carolinas (using a three-finger style banjoist) back in the early 1930s, before the Monroe Brothers were much of anything in that area. Story was a fiddler back then but later switched to the guitar and has made some worthy music over the years in both the gospel and secular fields of bluegrass. Somewhere along the line it was decided that playing a straight gospel format was an easier way to stay on the road, and Carl made the conversion and became a master of the demanding art of bluegrass gospel quartet singing.

Carl Story is probably the only countertenor in bluegrass. His voice is truly amazing: a rich bass-baritone at natural range, he shoots up to an otherworldly falsetto on the vocal choruses in a way that is both warm and chilling. The records he made with his Rambling Mountaineers for Mercury twenty years ago still rank with the best of a very difficult singing style, and many of the musicians who passed through his band on their way to stardom or oblivion were among the best, including mandolin whiz-kid Red Rector, fiddler Clarence "Tater" Tate, banjoist Bobby Thompson, and a great duet called the Brewster Brothers.

Story had his band way back when Mainer's Mountaineers were popular, and he has outlived all the old-time bands and many newer ones while keeping his standards high. Much of his fame is in the many fine gospel songs he has contributed to bluegrass, including the evergreens "Light at the

River," "Are You Afraid to Die?" "God Put a Rainbow in the Clouds," "Echoes from the Burning Bush," "No End to Heaven," and "My Lord Keeps a Record." It's fairly certain that if the Lord keeps a collection of bluegrass records, Carl Story's are among them.

There were other bands, too, who made a living out of playing both sides of the bluegrass-gospel fence. Back in the old days family groups were especially popular, probably due to the fame and success of the Carters. There were the Masters Family, the Phipps Family, the Raney Family, and the Leary Family. Later, when bluegrass had become established, there were the Sullivan Family and "The First Family of Gospel Song," the Lewis Family.

Georgians Pop Lewis and his family bring a bit of glamor as well as a heavy dose of deep southern warmth and charm to a field that has always been dominated by the middle sound of the central mountains. The band has always consisted of Pop and various combinations of his seven children. The gospel singing convention, camp meeting, and revival tent were their stomping grounds until they hit the festival circuit in 1970, when they virtually swept everyone off their benches, lawn chairs, and apple crates. The Lewis Family spent most of the 1950s and 1960s playing to the religious crowd on the same stage with less rural-sounding groups: those barber shop gospel groups who charm the audience with insincere smiles, slicked hair, and pencil-line moustaches. The Lewises had to rely on showmanship to win over the nonbluegrass audience, and they developed a dynamite show in the process. They secured a long-standing TV show in Augusta (now syndicated) and signed a contract with Starday records.

The band is a knockout on stage. Pop's three daughters, Miggie, Polly, and Janis sport bouffant hairdos and stage-length dresses. Pop plays the bass; the eldest son, Wallace, emcees and sings and plays rhythm guitar. The youngest son, Roy, is an instrumental dynamo. He is a fine bluegrass banjo picker and also is a nonstop comedian. The show moves as all six Lewises sing in various combinations and "Little" Roy provides an endless stream of jokes and insults in a thick Georgia accent that keeps the crowd supremely entertained.

Says "Little" Roy of his balding older brother, "Some people's hair turns gray. Wallace's done turned loose!"

Of his matronly older sister, Miggie, "Miggie's on a seafood diet. Every time she sees food, she eats it."

Of a portly man in the audience, "See that heavy man out there, Wallace?

I think he done got Dunlap's disease. His stomach done laps over his pants."

It's corny, but when Pop Lewis asks the audience, "Have you enjoyed the Lewis Family?" the response is generally deafening. The gospel field has been good to the hard-working Lewis Family, as may be seen by the crowd lined up at their record table after each of their shows.

Religious music has kept scores of good bluegrass musicians and their families fed and clothed, but others have had to rely on different means. Some had a keen business sense to fall back on, like Cincinnati's Jimmie Skinner, part owner of a thriving music business in that Ohio River city. Skinner is an older man, one of the followers of the Jimmie Rodgers school, never a hard-line bluegrass musician. He straddled the fence between bluegrass and old-time electric hillbilly music, but he occupies a spot in the hearts of most traditionalists for the relaxed country warmth of his style and the many fine songs he has contributed to the bluegrass song bag. Songs like "Will You Be Satisfied That Way?" "Don't Give Your Heart to a Rambler," and the classic "Doin' My Time." His old Mercury record of Bill Browning's "Dark Hollow" is the model most bluegrass singers used when learning it, and the song has been elevated to almost cliché status in the bluegrass ranks.

Mac Wiseman is another astute businessman who kept bread on his table through the fat and lean years by using a keen sense of where and when to invest money. The rotund Virginia balladeer was one of the important names in the early days, having been part of Molly O'Day's group before joining Flatt and Scruggs for their first recordings in 1948 and Bill Monroe for his last Columbia sessions in 1949. His own bluegrass group was organized shortly after he left Monroe. He took them to the "Louisiana Hayride" and a contract with Dot Records for a string of 78s that were among the most important of the early bluegrass releases. The Dot records, solid bluegrass, established Wiseman as one of the top dogs: "'Tis Sweet to Be Remembered," "I'll Still Write Your Name in the Sand," "Remembering," "I Wonder How the Old Folks Are at Home," and "Dreaming of a Little Cabin." He later moved the act to the "Old Dominion Barn Dance" in Richmond, becoming (in the mid-1950s) one of the most popular bluegrass singers of the day, as the "Barn Dance" was broadcast all over the East.

When the hard times came, the wily Wiseman was ready. He had groomed his image as a solo singer, fairly independent of band or backup, so when he was no longer able to carry a full band, Mac hit the road as a single. One person—even one of Wiseman's girth—was cheaper to feed than five. When the market for all traditional music finally collapsed, Wiseman simply left the performing end and became an executive for Dot Records in Los Angeles.

But for Mac Wiseman, a veteran showman even before joining the bluegrass ranks, staying away from the stage and the applause was not easy. The folk music revival provided him with a springboard back into the public eye, and he came out on Capitol Records with a few worthy efforts that emphasized the folk aspects of the Wiseman sound. The situation led to a spot on the WWVA "Jamboree," not only as the show's principal star but also as program director, director of the talent agency, and owner of the late-night "record shop" program, which specialized in mail-order record sales.

The move to Wheeling coincided with the birth of the bluegrass festivals, and the shrewd Wiseman became a bluegrass singer once again, although he was never again to tour with his own band. The next move was to RCA in Nashville, where he teamed with Lester Flatt for three successful reunion albums, and then to Kentucky, where he started his own bluegrass festival at the site of the historic "Renfro Valley Barn Dance."

The choice of the Renfro Valley site for a festival was a good illustration of Wiseman's insight and business sense. The old "Barn Dance" programs, originated by a legendary figure named John Lair, were broadcast through the 1940s and are fondly remembered by thousands, especially in that rich Kentucky migration country of southern and central Ohio. Many attend Mac Wiseman's festival and other Renfro Valley get-togethers for reasons purely sentimental. Sentimentality has long been a part of Wiseman's trade, earning him the nickname of The Voice with a Heart.

There were other bands, too, who waded into bluegrass while wisely choosing to avoid the total plunge. One of the best was Wilma Lee and Stoney Cooper and their Clinch Mountain Clan, now members of the "Grand Ole Opry." Wilma Lee was a member of West Virginia's gospel-singing Leary Family before marrying the group's fiddler, Stoney Cooper. Their style paralleled bluegrass for many years, using the sounds of the fiddle, banjo, and dobro to augment their singing and electric instruments. Many of the better bluegrass sidemen passed through their band, including banjoists Johnny Clark and Vic Jordan, fiddler Tex Logan, and the greatest of all the dobro players, Buck Graves.

The Louvin Brothers were another act who kept a toe in the door of bluegrass and traditional music while relying on the sounds of electric instruments and the spangled costumes of Nashville. They were the last of the great guitar-mandolin brother acts in "straight" country music, and their music of the 1950s was based strongly on the sounds of the Bailes Brothers, the Blue Sky Boys, and similar groups. It is often said of the Louvins that they would have been shattering as a bluegrass duet. Ira Louvin's tenor voice and mandolin playing were pure bluegrass, even though his instrumental technique wasn't flashy. Much the same could be said for the talents of younger brother, Charlie, but it was in the field of songwriting that they were really outstanding. Their songs had many of the qualities that appealed to the bluegrass listener, and while they themselves never recorded in bluegrass style, they were about as close as anyone could come to it without actually wearing the label.

The bluegrass bands were quick to learn the Louvin songs, and their material continues to be a vital part of the bluegrass repertoire, even though Ira has been dead for more than a decade. Songs like "When I Stop Dreaming," "Alabama," "Childish Love," "The Weapon of Prayer," "Here Today and Gone Tomorrow," "Make Him a Soldier," "Cash on the Barrelhead," "The Seven-Year Blues," "You're Running Wild," "The Get-Acquainted Waltz," "Are You Missing Me?" and "Love and Wealth" are all among the standards of bluegrass.

The Louvin Brothers would probably have gone into bluegrass if they had thought they could make a living at it. Similar statements have been heard from Nashville superstars Porter Wagoner and George Jones, both of whom openly cite Bill Monroe as one of their principal inspirations. But neither would be where he is today if he had pursued a career in bluegrass.

Others were impressed so strongly by bluegrass and Bill Monroe that they could follow no other course than the pure sounds of the fiddle, banjo, and mandolin. Red Allen was one, as were the Lilly Brothers, Earl Taylor, Connie and Babe (or Connie and Joe), the Lonesome Pine Fiddlers, and dozens of others. Some made it to the big leagues—the major record labels—only to find that the companies were not willing to push bluegrass and would not keep the records in print. The story was repeated as one band after another descended from their spots near the top and settled into that miserable life of the dismal bars, many times playing long nights for less than a hundred dollars.

Hylo Brown made it to a big label (Capitol) and was able to record some great bluegrass while he was there. A superb album and some singles were made while he was touring with his Timberliners under the Martha White banner in the late 1950s. But the Martha White deal eroded, the band disintegrated, the Capitol deal fell through, and Brown has since been batted around in the fray.

The Lilly Brothers, who are the most gently old-time-sounding of all the bluegrass duets, were once members of the WWVA "Jamboree" before brother Everett joined Flatt and Scruggs as mandolinist, helping record some of their best material of the early 1950s—"'Tis Sweet to be Remembered," "I'm Gonna Settle Down," "Get in Line, Brother," "I'm Working on a Road," "Over the Hill to the Poor House," "Earl's Breakdown," and many others of equal distinction. Everett and his brother Mitchell "Bea" moved to Boston to play with fiddler Tex Logan (then attending MIT) and banjoist Don Stover, and there they stayed for almost twenty years, playing nightly in a bar called the Hillbilly Ranch. Much of the current popularity of bluegrass in New England stems from the Lillys, but many of the fans who made pilgrimages to see them came away heartsick. Above the drunken sailors, whores, fights, and noise stood the Lillys and Don Stover, playing their hearts out, staring misty-eyed into the cigarette smoke that clung to the ceiling, trying to imagine themselves away from the beer garden and back in their native West Virginia mountains. The Lilly Brothers, unfortunately, are typical.

Earl Taylor now plays the bars in Cincinnati. He had been one of the top bluegrass bandleaders. He and his Stony Mountain Boys once played Carnegie Hall in New York, and there were some fine records for Capitol and United Artists. But now Taylor makes it when he can and when he has the band, his enormously powerful tenor voice and Monroe-style mandolin undaunted.

The first time I saw Bill Monroe, "live and in person," was unforgettable. It was 1963, and I had been preparing myself for weeks. I had worshiped the man, stayed up many school nights playing his records at a speed so slow that the words and songs could barely be understood, in order to pick out the notes he was playing on his mandolin. I pictured a godlike man, bigger than life, and I wasn't disappointed. He was everything I had hoped for.

The place was a well-known folk coffeehouse out in West Hollywood called the Ash Grove. It wasn't a dump, but the atmosphere was intentionally raunchy and many of those who frequented the place were still referred to as beatniks. The first thing that impressed me upon walking up the back street and through the little service station parking lot was the

TWENTY-FIVE YEARS OF HUNGRY BLUEGRASS

Bluegrass Special, a grimy monster of a bullet-back road bus that probably dated back to 1948. The inside was a jumble of dirty laundry strewn over torn, stained seats, and Bill Monroe's name was painted on the back with what looked like a toothbrush dipped in india ink.

The show was great—he had Del McCoury, Bill Keith, Billy Baker, and Bessie Lee Mauldin with him—but the audience wasn't. Most didn't know who he was. Someone in the audience yelled for Bill to do "Scotch and Soda," one of the Kingston Trio's big numbers. Bill patiently answered that he didn't know the tune. A woman sitting near me whispered to her escort that Monroe's voice sounded so "high and funny." Seeing Bill up there, unappreciated, was one of the really depressing events of my young life, and I could instantly relate to the hundreds of other lesser bands who were playing, probably at that very moment, under conditions far worse and getting paid considerably less for their trouble.

I didn't see the real point of the incident until years later, when I was in the army. I heard Bill on a segment of the "Opry" that Armed Forces Radio broadcast every Saturday night, and I thought back to that night at the Ash Grove. Out of the eighty-plus people in the room that night, only about a fourth of them knew of Bill Monroe and his music, and few of those worshiped the man as I did. But yet, there we were, about as far away from the southern mountains as you can get, sitting in a hip coffeehouse in the middle of Los Angeles, and there were a few people there who really flipped over Bill Monroe and bluegrass. They called up his old songs: "Good-Bye, Old Pal," "Heavy Traffic Ahead," "Can't You Hear Me Calling?" and "Bluegrass Ramble."

There is something about this man and his music that hits certain people a certain way, that makes them fanatics. It happened to Pee Wee Lambert. It happened to Red Allen. It happened to Jimmy Martin, it happened to the Stanley Brothers and to the Lilly Brothers. It happened to me, just as it had happened to a half-dozen others who were at the Ash Grove that night. It was probably happening to one or two while we were sitting there. Geography and background obviously had nothing to do with it, nor did age, sex, politics, or religion. There is just something about the high wail of the harmony, the tight-lipped intensity of the musicians, and the blur of fast fingers on strings that hits some sensitive people. They are never the same again.

If a large percentage of the people who *were* exposed to it were thrilled to the point of possession, what could happen if bluegrass got just one shot at the national market? Most people would hate it, their minds closed to anything that smacks of the barnyard. But surely enough would love it and be moved by it to make a difference in the overall music picture.

My attitude in the early 1960s was that everyone should at least have the chance to hear it, to accept it or reject it. It crossed my teen-age mind also that someone, probably Nashville, was sitting on the lid of a carefully sealed Pandora's box, with the frustration and heartache of all those years with bluegrass, all those old records waiting to be heard, all the great fiddles and banjos and supreme musicianship sealed inside. As the next few years passed, there were developments that convinced me that the contents of the box couldn't be contained much longer. The word was slowly leaking to the outside world.

10

Newgrass and the Country Gentlemen

THE WASHINGTON SOUND

A Canadian fan once remarked after reading the club listings in *Bluegrass Unlimited* magazine that the area around Washington and Baltimore seemed like a bluegrass heaven. Dozens of clubs feature as many bands, great and not so great, in that small section surrounding the nation's capital.

Washington is by no means typical. In most cities, one good (or even mediocre) bluegrass band is considered a boon. Residents of Cleveland or St. Paul wonder how one area can support so much bluegrass activity; deciding which band to go see on any given night would be a nearly impossible task, one even the most avid enthusiast in one of the many "dry" areas could not imagine ever facing. The Washington area has become the hub of the entire bluegrass movement.

Why and how? Those aren't easily answered questions. Why did Nashville become the country music capital? How did Hollywood become the home of the movies?

Just as the big migration of the 1920s was toward the golden shores of the West, much of the post-World War II migration was from South to North. The North had heavy industry and jobs; jobs for those Carolinians and Kentuckians with thick mountain accents, limited education, and hungry kids. Some moved to Detroit, Chicago, and Columbus; others moved to Philadelphia, Baltimore, and the District of Columbia. As mountain families moved and settled into the new life, friends and relatives back home were encouraged to come up and enjoy the bounties of suburban homes and steady incomes. Most of the heavy population centers in the North became bluegrass centers as the culture of the immigrants was infused into the strange new surroundings.

The smoke and soot of the average northern city is far removed from the clean air and forests of the southern mountains. But air and mountains can't be fed to the kids, and they came north in an endless stream to make cars in Detroit and Flint, detergent in Cincinnati, appliances in Dayton, tires in Akron, and steel in Pittsburgh. But it was hard to take two hundred years of the West Virginia hollows out of a man's blood, especially when most of his new northern neighbors were from Sandy Hook, Kentucky, and Grundy, Virginia. The accents stayed the same, and so did the music.

A Kentucky fiddler working in a General Motors assembly plant would try to locate other musicians on the job; a guitarist and singer first, then a banjo picker, bass player, and maybe someone who knew a few tunes on a mandolin or dobro. They'd get together on weekends or after work and play music—the music they grew up with and were most comfortable with, the stuff they'd heard Bill Monroe and the others play on the radio.

Bluegrass was played in factory parking lots at lunchtime and in garages and kitchens at night while cold beer was sipped and the wives sat in the other room talking about mutual friends and relatives back home. If the makeshift bluegrass band was good enough, its members might try to pick a name, something appropriately mountain-sounding, like the "Blue Ridge Mountain Boys," and they would make the rounds of the local beer joints looking for work at forty or fifty bucks total. A few of the clubs, the ones with hillbillies as regular patrons, might hire them for Saturday night.

The pattern was repeated endlessly in town after town: Wherever more than fifty immigrant "briarhoppers" would congregate, there would be a bluegrass band. In those awkward years between rock 'n' roll's devastating ascent and the big folk music revival, bluegrass was gasping for breath in the smokiest, noisiest, roughest bars in the worst neighborhoods of the big cities of the North.

The classic bluegrass bar was a dismal affair. There were probably hundreds of them across the northeastern quarter of the United States, each a carbon copy of the others. Nights without a fight or a knifing were a rarity. The mountain men still held to the lawless ways of the hills. Just for a little color, let's spend a night in one of the bars. It could be in any city, the year about 1958.

NEWGRASS AND THE COUNTRY GENTLEMEN

The street is dark and many of the buildings are boarded up. There is no parking anywhere, so we have to park several blocks away, by the side of the loading dock of an abandoned warehouse. There are no street lights. It's one of the oldest industrial neighborhoods in the city, and no one comes down here at night unless he has specific business. Our business is to find a little bar where there's reported to be a good bluegrass band.

There are three bars on this street, and they all look alike. We've been told that the one we want is in the middle of the block. It sports a sign, "THE WELCOME INN," supplied by the local Coca-Cola distributor. The windows on either side of the padded front door are heavy glass block, surrounded by flickering red neon that looks in danger of quitting at any moment. Several glass blocks are cracked and broken, and we can speculate that either stones or bullets were responsible. The sputtering neon letters across one of the windows shriek "BEER"; the other side spells "SAND-WICHES." The gray stucco facade is about fifteen years overdue for renovation.

Inside, the noise level is ear-splitting. The bartender, dangling a cigarette, bellows for a sodden customer to leave. The man insists he's sober, twirls angrily on the torn leatherette barstool to leave, and falls on his face. Somebody laughs, but no one offers assistance.

The wooden bar runs the length of the left wall, and the rough-looking patrons are lined up three and four deep. It's dark and the air is thick with cigarette smoke, but there is the look of the mountains in the faces at the bar. The old men are sunken-eyed and slack-jawed and they wear rumpled baseball caps; the younger men wear T-shirts and crew cuts with Elvis-length sideburns. The place is dirty, and as our eyes adjust to the dark we see that the walls are stained and the ceiling is mottled with rust-colored water marks. The floor in front of the bar, what we can see of it, is covered with cigarette butts and peanut shells.

It's stuffy. The chairs don't match, but they are painted the same shade of chipped red. There are about seven round tables out in the center of the room, all occupied. There are no tablecloths and some of the tables have two or three pitchers of beer on them. There is a light in the back corner, a spotlight, and on stage, barely big enough to accommodate them, stand four men in their early thirties wearing short-sleeved, tab-collar dress shirts. This is the band we have come to see.

A stocky man with a broken nose and tennis-ball haircut lovingly uncases a guitar—a big, battered Martin with several scratches across the top. The top has mellowed from its original white wood color to a deep patina. A thin man, younger than the others, tries to tune a cheap-model Gibson mandolin while a bored-looking banjo picker leans languidly against the back wall, playing softly to himself, waiting for something to happen. A fat guy with horn-rimmed glasses holds a bass fiddle while joking with the waitress, and the guitar man adjusts the microphone and puts a metal, spring-action capo on the second fret of his guitar. The banjo player attaches his capo accordingly, searches his pockets for finger picks, and the four of them get ready for the first song.

The banjo player stands close to the mike and starts to play as loud and as hard as he can, trying to push the sound over the din of the crowd. It's fast, and the mandolin player is playing a "chomp" closed chord while the guitarist swoops down on the rhythm like a locomotive. The cheap, ancient PA system distorts the sound, and the only ones getting a true version of what the music sounds like are the fortunates at the two nearest tables. The bass is heard in all four corners of the room, sending a booming, in-time thump behind the ensemble. The banjo puts in one or two special licks the picker knows always gets the crowd on his side, and the ring and the drive are enough to make half the audience let out bloodcurdling rebel yells and start some doing a drunken version of the old mountain "buck 'n' wing" clog dance.

It was a good banjo kick-off, and the crowd is temporarily theirs, although few in the room realize how long it took, how many years, to get that sound from a banjo—the Earl Scruggs sound. The guitar man steps up to the mike and sends the banjo man out of his break with a run on the bass strings, the one Lester Flatt popularized and Red Smiley perfected. He starts singing in a strong voice that's a noticeable takeoff on the loud, cocky growl of Jimmy Martin. The song is one of Bill Monroe's, "I'm on My Way Back to the Old Home," and a few in the crowd listen and realize that the song was written about them, or people like them. Monroe wrote the song after he had left the little town of Rosine, Kentucky, where he was born. He, too, went north to find work in the big refineries, and the song tells of going home and finding no lights in the windows—everyone has either moved away or died. Few in the audience are sober or sensitive enough to sense the irony in the fact that words with such a tragic message are being sung to music that is so buoyantly alive.

Most don't even hear the words of the song. It's so fast, such a fleeting

110

series of banjo and mandolin breaks and verses and choruses that the message is lost on them. They're just caught up in the good feel of the music. As the last chorus comes up, the mandolin player leans in from the left to sing the high tenor and the banjo man leans in from the back to sing the third part. The three of them sing into the one little mike, and their harmony is high, clear, and loud. The song ends, there are more rebel yells, and a few people applaud. Most resume their drinking and will pay little attention for the rest of the evening.

There are two college kids at one of the front tables, obviously out of place and unquestionably too young to be in a bar. Their attention is glued to the stage as they timidly nurse bottles of beer and drink in every note the musicians play. One of them has just bought a used Gibson mandolin, the other a used five-string, and they've come down here to listen and learn. They will probably go home tonight and stay up 'til dawn trying to remember the songs and licks, and within a year or two they might be good enough to have their own little bluegrass band. But theirs will play at the campus coffeehouse to a more attentive crowd, and they will probably turn several of their contemporaries on to the hard, lonesome sounds of bluegrass.

The band we've come to see is slightly better than most. They know their stuff and will proceed to prove it in the course of four forty-five-minute sets. We realize that they really have to love it to put up with the squalor and aggravation. The crowd is several times more boisterous than what could be considered reasonable, and the PA setup is so bad that if the volume is turned up high enough to penetrate the noise, the cheap, wall-mounted speakers will squeal like air-raid sirens.

Undaunted, they sing. There's an appropriately bluesy version of Flatt and Scruggs' "Dim Lights, Thick Smoke" and a reverent version of the Stanleys' hymnlike "White Dove," which seems totally out of place in these surroundings. Then they jump back into the fast stuff with a tear-'em-up version of Don Reno's "Chokin' the Strings." Amidst all the beautiful bluegrass, one couple insists that they do one of the current country hits, a slow thing that's been popular on the jukebox for several months. They sing it, grudgingly, while the banjo player struggles with the slow tempo. The couple glides around the floor between the tables. The two college kids view the whole thing with distaste as the singers end their abbreviated rendition with a slow, fancy ending like they've heard the Osborne Brothers and Red Red Allen do over at WWVA.

111

BLUEGRASS

They've made the dancing couple happy, but the banjo player doesn't look too pleased. He whispers something into the guitar man's ear, the capos are removed, and the banjo man steps up and lays into an Earl Scruggs instrumental with a vengeance. It's the "Flint Hill Special."

The college kid who has the banjo is staring in disbelief as part of the tune is played by actually retuning the banjo in the middle of the song. A mechanical gadget is the secret, an invention called "twisters" or "cheaters" down in the Carolinas, enabling the instrumentalist to swing from G to D tuning with a characteristic *boing* sound. The young banjoist will scour the music stores on Monday looking for a set of twisters, but he'll end up making a pair out of household nuts and bolts. Music stores don't carry such exotic stuff.

It's now one o'clock, and the bar is practically empty. The college kids are still here, now loosened up by the three bottles of beer they've each consumed, and they're requesting songs. The band is glad that someone out in the darkness that surrounds the stage knows something about bluegrass, and they can tell that the kids have been doing their homework by tuning in Reno and Smiley from WRVA down in Richmond, Flatt and Scruggs at the "Opry," and the Osbornes over in Wheeling.

The bartender is still here, and so is the drunk who comes in twice a week to clean the place in exchange for a few drinks. He's putting chairs up on the tables and wishing the band would go home so he could finish up and get his free shot of booze. The bartender sends up a silent signal for the band to quit.

The guy behind the bar is a tough-looking man with scars across the ridge of his brow, the sign of his profession. He's not smiling, in the knowledge that he's only sold two bottles of beer in the past half hour. He motions, and the guitar man, who has been singing his heart out for the last four hours, raises the mike up to mouth level and says, with all the aplomb of an "Opry" star, that it's been a real pleasure playing for everyone and "Y'all come back next week, 'hear?" at which the banjo player lays into the "Bluegrass Breakdown" and the two college kids applaud like they've been sitting in the front row balcony at Carnegie Hall.

The mention that the band might be here next week causes the guy behind the bar to scowl at them as he counts the money in the cash drawer. He and the guitar man exchange sour looks through the cigarette haze, which still lingers even though the last smoker left an hour ago.

The instruments are cased, the mike laid carefully to rest, and the guitar man braces himself with a last drag on a now-warm beer before walking over to the bar to settle the night's business. Playing in a place like this is bad enough, but doing business with the owner is worse.

"How'd we do?" asks the guitar man, referring to the evening's intake of cash.

" 'We' didn't do so good. You guys ain't holdin' the crowd. The people who do come to see you ain't buyin' booze, and we can't break even on draft beer."

"Now, wait a minute. I know that the boys and I done spent about ten bucks on beer between us. That's a quarter of what we make here, and I just can't believe that you ain't makin' money."

"I got bills to pay. I'll let you look at 'em sometime. I can't afford you guys—I got an electric band plays country music here on Tuesday nights, and they play for nothin' but free drinks, and they give the crowd what they want to hear. You know, that loud, jukebox stuff."

"Well," retaliates the guitar man, "there's hardly any place in town that has what we play, bluegrass music, and if people knew we was here, they'd come to hear us. We been spreadin' the word around, but you have to push some, too. Advertise it."

"I can't afford it. I can't afford you, either. So I'm comin' down five bucks on your price and movin' you to Wednesday, because my Saturday night regulars are leavin' and goin' to the place down the street where they can dance. So if you want to come back Wednesday, fine. If not, don't."

The college kids pass the bar and the bartender musters a smile and says, "Good night. Come back next week and bring your girls. We'll have a *real* band then." The young banjo player shoots a surprised look at the guitar man, who doesn't return the look.

This story is typical. That was the way it was through most of the 1950s (and still is in many places) for nearly every bluegrass band. A "straight" country band didn't have it much better, but at least if they worked hard enough and became good enough they could take it somewhere, to one of the "Opry" bush leagues like Wheeling, or the "Louisiana Hayride" in Shreveport. Being a regular on one of those respected shows could lead to something—to Nashville and the really big money. The best the bluegrass musician could do was to shoot for the day when one of the big bluegrass bands had an opening, to play with Monroe, or Mac Wiseman, or maybe someone like Hylo Brown. But to take the band itself somewhere—no, it just couldn't be done. They'd have to stick it out in the bars if they wanted to keep playing the music they loved.

For a few of the bands the bar jobs were at least steady. The Lilly Brothers and Don Stover played nightly for eighteen years at the Hillbilly Ranch in Boston, and Mac Martin and his band, the Dixie Travelers, played at a place called Walsh's in Pittsburgh every week for over fifteen years. And there was the Astro Inn in Columbus, which frequently booked the major bands. Then there was Washington, D.C.

Good bluegrass musicians seemed to throng to (and thrive in) the capital city. There were probably more good bands and musicians in south-central Ohio, but they were spread over a wide area, from Cincinnati to Youngstown, and from Portsmouth up through Akron and Cleveland. But in the East they were crammed into one small area around the District of Columbia, the northernmost part of Virginia, and into Maryland and Delaware.

Outstanding musicians would jump from band to band, sometimes in the same week. Banjoist Porter Church, Tom Morgan and the Yates Brothers, Smiley Hobbs, Pete Roberts, Scott Stoneman, Kenny Haddock—they would bring their talent and ideas to a band, learn something from the musicians already there, and leave something of their musical personality when they left. If a band member quit, it was no problem to get on the phone and have a replacement within hours. By the middle of the 1950s there was probably more professional-quality bluegrass being played in the bars around Washington than on the top three country music "jamborees" combined.

The bands abounded. There was Buzz Busby, a fine mandolin player and singer, and there was a band called the Blue Grass Champs, which went on to much fame as the Stoneman Family. Earl Taylor played there with his band, the Stony Mountain Boys, and Red Allen moved in after leaving the Osborne Brothers. And there were Bill Harrell, and Bennie and Vallie Cain, and Bill Clifton, who became one of the most popular bluegrass bandleaders through his Starday records and use of top sidemen. Young Mike Seeger, a member of the famous folk music family, played with some of the Baltimore bands and immortalized the best of them in his historic Folkways anthology recording, "Mountain Music, Bluegrass Style."

One band that was formed on the Fourth of July, 1957, was probably the most influential band ever to be born of the bluegrass bar tradition. It started at a club outside Washington called the Admiral Grill. Buzz Busby's group had been the featured band, and when Busby was hurt in an auto wreck, banjoist Bill Emerson got on the phone and contacted some other musicians to help him hold down the job. He got a guitarist who had played with Busby as well as Earl Taylor, a guy from Louisiana named Charlie Waller. Then he contacted a mandolinist named John Duffey, whose opera-singing father had taught him how to send his tenor voice up through the clouds and whose flashy mandolin playing was gaining local fame. A bass player was located, and after a few weeks they realized that they were really clicking. They sought a name and found one that fit the sound: the Country Gentlemen.

The Country Gentlemen has been a uniformly superb band since the first. Two or three banjo players bounced in and out of the group before they settled on a Virginian named Eddie Adcock, who had played with Mac Wiseman. Their trio was sterling, and it was not the bluegrass trio almost everyone had been accustomed to. Theirs were three thoroughly unique voices that happened to mesh into one of the two or three best bluegrass trios ever assembled. Waller had a voice that was technically better than the average bluegrass singer, sort of a cross between country singer Hank Snow and the least bluegrass aspects of Mac Wiseman. He was much more of a vocalist than the usual bluegrass "bellower," and his diction and pronunciation were better than that of a lot of popular singers of the day. Duffey, possibly the loudest tenor in bluegrass, had little of that high, nasal quality to his voice. It wasn't operatic, but it was full and rich, not the flat, twangy sound so many associate with the tenor singing of bluegrass. Adcock's warbling baritone was hushed and breathy, complimenting Duffey's unique voice and making their trio truly one of a kind.

Their instrumentation was equally unique. Duffey and Adcock were a pair of creative pickers, and their specific aim was to dazzle, to be a little different, to do something out of the ordinary. They succeeded, with Adcock elaborating on the wildest side of the Don Reno style and even adapting his own version of Travis-style guitar picking to the banjo. Nothing seemed beyond them as they recorded material on Starday, Folkways, Mercury—versions of the old jazz tunes "Bye Bye Blues" and "Heartaches," popular folk tunes like "Tom Dooley" and "Copper Kettle," and traditional bluegrass such as "Red Rockin' Chair," "Poor Ellen Smith," and "I'll Never Marry," all done in a slick, jazzy-but-fairly-straight blue-grass style that other bands and musicians would never have thought possible.

The Gentlemen were one of the first bands to have two sources of ideas. One, of course, was the world of straight bluegrass. The other was the then-hip world of folk music. They were tradition-oriented enough to seek out some of the best- and least-known songs of traditional bands like the Stanley Brothers and give that material a sophisticated rearranging. But they also had an ear for the trends of popular music, much of it thoroughly adaptable to bluegrass. From the Kingston Trio came the tradition-flavored "Brown Mountain Light," from Harry Belafonte came the unlikely "Banana Boat Song," and from the pen of Shel Silverstein came the riotous "Big Bruce," a homosexual takeoff on Jimmy Dean's hit country song "Big John." Their style matured even further as they joined the Washington-based Rebel label in the mid-1960s.

Waller, Duffey, Adcock, and their bassists (the best remembered of whom was Tom Gray) had a lot more going for them than a hip musical attitude. Their personalities seemed to mesh. They were three aspects of one musical personality, and that was one of their greatest strengths, especially as a stage band. No one who saw one of their stage shows can forget the experience.

Their aim was to sell their music to people—not just to the bluegrass people but to anyone who happened to be in the audience. Their choice of material was one indication of their reaching for new and wider audiences, and their stage show was enough to sway even the most staunchly an-tibluegrass fanatic over into the camp. Waller had a been-through-it-all face, always ready with a wide smile and subtle wit. John Duffey had a wisecracking sense of humor, coupled with a Monroevian arrogance, and would force feed his genius-laden mandolin licks to his listeners with a like-it-or-else grin. Adcock was a natural comic, jumping, stomping, mugging, and generally clowning.

The classic Gentlemen routine was their flaky takeoff on the standard "Duelin' Banjos." The point of the song is, of course, to have two of the instruments swap licks, to try to outdazzle each other. By the time the Gentlemen got hold of the number, almost everything that could have been done with it had been done, so they decided to poke a little fun. They would clown, jump around, dance with each other, Waller would sneak in a fancy guitar break in defiance of the others' insistence that the guitar was only intended for rhythm. They would chase each other, often sending Adcock off the edge of the stage, banjo and all, with a resounding Johnny Weissmuller ape call. Then someone would get the idea to finally outdo the others by playing the instrument behind his head—first Adcock (of course), then Duffey and Waller. The crowning touch was when their spherical bass player, Ed Ferris, was intimidated into lifting the big bass onto his shoulders, backwards, never missing a beat as he, too, played behind his head. In a field where the musicians were almost universally depicted as sullen and soulful, the effect was more than funny. It was irreverent, and the irreverence was part of what the Country Gentlemen were.

To other musicians, one of the funniest numbers was their spoof of "Cripple Creek," traditionally the tune that most bluegrass musicians learn first by taking a 33⅓ rpm record and slowing it down to the next speed. The result is a deep, bassy, draggy growl with each note played with a painful deliberateness. It is the only way beginners can pick out all the notes of a fast banjo tune, and when the Gentlemen kicked it off on stage, it received instant recognition from all the musicians in the audience. They even slow-growled the first verse in three-part harmony.

Except, possibly, for Flatt and Scruggs, the Country Gentlemen made more bluegrass converts than anyone. In terms of bringing in new fans who had always been disdainful of the raw hillbilly aspects of bluegrass, they undoubtedly did as much as Flatt and Scruggs. In 1969 they were the only name act at the festivals who could consistently bring the audience to its feet. That same year, John Duffey left.

Duffey was the artistic backbone of the Gentlemen sound, and his leaving raised a few doubts as to their ability to carry on without him. But carry on they did, replacing the inimitable mandolin wizard with a youngster from Rhode Island named Jimmy Gaudreau. John Duffey had acquired quite a following, and a lot of kids were spending their time playing *his* records at slow speed. Gaudreau's accent was strictly New England, but his music was pure Country Gentlemen, and the band didn't drop a single note in a quick period of readjustment.

Then Adcock left Washington, to be replaced by the original Gentlemen banjoist, Bill Emerson. Emerson had been making a name for himself, along with his partner Cliff Waldron, as one of the up-and-coming bands of the new progressive movement in bluegrass, and his singing, arranging, and banjo playing were decided plusses, even though the old Country Gentlemen personality mesh wasn't there. But they did a fantastic job of glossing it over with sheer professionalism.

Even before Duffey and Adcock left, they had started a movement. They were playing a new kind of bluegrass that most were calling progressive. A lot of people saw this as the next evolutionary phase in the long story of bluegrass, and other bands were following it. There was, of course, controversy. Some people had turned to bluegrass in the first place because they didn't want things to change. After all, regular country music had changed right out from under them in the 1950s, and bluegrass had been their refuge. Now there was turmoil again, and the Country Gentlemen were right at the center. Like it or not, there was a revolution afoot in bluegrass, and it was all happening in Washington, D.C.

Good things were happening in the old town. In 1966 a little mimeographed magazine began appearing in the festival parking lots and in people's mailboxes. Called *Bluegrass Unlimited*, it was distributed in the Washington area by a few enthusiastic bluegrass fans who felt there was enough action around to warrant a clearinghouse. The magazine rose rapidly from a stapled, mimeographed newsletter to a small, printed booklet, and it had some very well-informed people writing for it. Within a few years it had gone beyond Washington and was becoming the national voice of bluegrass. Red Allen reviewed records, authorities like Richard K. Spottswood reviewed festivals, and John Duffey gave advice on how to keep guitar bridges from falling off. The magazine also provided bluegrass with its first forum, and much of the bluegrass controversy was spread across its pages: Should the Osbornes have gone electric? Who was right in that silly feud between Jimmy Martin and Carlton Haney? Lester and Earl? What *really* happened between Reno and Smiley? It was just what the long-displaced bluegrass fans had been looking for, and it grew. Just as the "Grand Ole Opry" had helped make Nashville the country music capital, *Bluegrass Unlimited* (with its sometimes ill-concealed local bias) helped make Washington the bluegrass capital, or at least solidify the lead it already had over other areas.

Bluegrass Unlimited gave rise to other publications. Festival impresario Carlton Haney started his *Muleskinner News*, wisely putting it into the editorial hands of the talented and energetic Fred Bartenstein. There were a few on the West Coast, and James Monroe (Bill's singing son) started one called the *Bluegrass Star* in Nashville. All served to unify the bluegrass world, to channel things into a single direction, to bring people together with their new or old ideas, and to let the rest of the world know there was something going on in the music world that could support enough subscribers to keep three or four magazines alive.

But Washington was acclaimed as the center of the bluegrass world, and while some would argue the point (Nashville, for example), it was a very real fact. *Bluegrass Unlimited* had given bluegrass a voice, and it was a Washington publication. The Country Gentlemen had aimed bluegrass in a new and valid direction, and they were a Washington group. A raft of magazines sprang up in the likeness of *BU*, and many bands started emulating the Country Gentlemen, in concept if not in actual style.

There was every indication that something was about to break, even as folk music was drifting off into history. Predictions were made that bluegrass would be the next big rage. But when? How long could the bands wait? When the break came, would it be for traditional bluegrass or the newer sounds? Many bands didn't wait to find out. Columbia was cranking out one soggy, overproduced Flatt and Scruggs LP after another, with Lester and the boys trying to sing material like Dylan's "Maggie's Farm." The Dillards, a fine Ozark bluegrass band that had become popular through appearances on the "Andy Griffith Show," had plugged in their banjos and mandolins and were playing California folk-rock. The Bray Brothers in Missouri were giving bluegrass a slick, new direction even before coming out with their well-remembered "Bluegrass Gents" LP on the Liberty label. Then there were Jim and Jesse, doing their best to keep from going under while singing electrified country songs about diesel trucks.

There were young bands coming along, too, since the late 1950s, and one of the first was a bunch of New Yorkers who called themselves the Greenbriar Boys. Guitarist John Herald, banjoist Bob Yellin, and mandolinist Eric Weissberg (who was to become better known as a banjoist even before his "Deliverance" record made him wealthy) were one of the first urban bluegrass bands, and their impact was felt in the cities. Weissberg was later replaced by mandolinist Ralph Rinzler, a major figure in the folk and bluegrass movements, partly through his association with Bill Monroe and his current role as director of the Folk Life Program at the Smithsonian Institution. The Greenbriar Boys gave the urban audience an urban interpretation of bluegrass, both in personal appearances and on their excellent Vanguard LPs, which later included some of the best "authentic" greats, like mandolinist Frank Wakefield and fiddler Jim Buchanan. When the jug band movement became the folk rage, parts of that style were found in the Greenbriars' music, displaying a sense of inventiveness that was later to be a hallmark of the progressive movement.

The magazines, the festivals, new bands of young men with new ideas—it was all leading somewhere. Bill Emerson and Cliff Waldron recorded "If I

Were a Carpenter" and "Fox on the Run." The post-Duffey and Adcock Country Gentlemen were recording the songs of James Taylor; Gordon Lightfoot; Crosby, Stills, Nash, and Young; and Simon and Garfunkel, and it was hailed as some of the best new stuff in bluegrass. Hair was getting longer as the sound and look of pop were seeping in. Red Allen's three sons, Harley, Greg, and Neal, were making excellent modern bluegrass with their father. Their shoulder-length-plus hair drew a great deal of comment, much of it from their own father.

John Hartford, a Missouri banjoist and fiddler, was making his own kind of personal music based on the straight bluegrass he once played. Some of the Nashville pickers were catching on with the younger crowd, men like the bearded Norman Blake and balding dobroist Tut Taylor. Youth was gradually being drawn in, and the sounds they brought with them were changing bluegrass more in a few years than it had changed in the last twenty.

Festival-goers were shocked when Carlton Haney and Fred Bartenstein began booking funky-dressed, shaggy-haired bands into their festivals. Many were outraged, many pleased, and everyone was impressed with the fact that things probably wouldn't be the same anymore. Entire festivals were booked to feature the most rock-oriented groups, drawing the most rock-oriented audiences. It was a movement within a movement. Just as bluegrass was given a name because it was something different from straight country music, with which it was often confused, so did the new movement need a name.

There was a band that appeared at one of the Carlton Haney festivals near Reidsville, North Carolina. It was a very good, folk-oriented band called the Bluegrass Alliance, and guesting with the group (which included fiddler Lonnie Pierce, bassist Ebo Walker, guitarists Dan Jones and Dan Crary, and banjoist Buddy Spurlock) was a teen-ager in blue jeans and T-shirt named Sam Bush. The band's success at the festival was seen in the applause that almost uprooted some of Haney's newly planted shade trees, instantly putting the Alliance at the top of the bluegrass best-new-band list. They carried a wallop and were seen as the next big bluegrass band. Crary, an astounding lead guitarist, left the band to study for the ministry in his native Kansas, and Jones left to eventually wind up with Bill Monroe for a few months. Walker and Bush formed a new band, based on the concepts of merging the sounds of the bluegrass instruments with the beat and feel of rock. They called their band the New Grass Revival.

It's still not clear (to me at least) whether the band drew its name from the movement or the movement from the band. It is clear, however, that by the early 1970s the movement had found a name: newgrass. New bluegrass. Today if someone says to a bearded, long-haired musician, "Son, that ain't bluegrass," the picker can look him straight in the eye, smile, and honestly say, "You're right," and go right on playing.

The members of the Revival (Walker, Bush, banjoist Courtney Johnson, and guitarist Curtis Burch) were from Kentucky, but the center was still well within the confines of the Washington area. Eddie Adcock reappeared, long-haired and bearded, to join Jimmy Gaudreau in a super-progressive band called the II Generation. Then Gaudreau left to join Keith Whitley (of Ralph Stanley fame) in a soft-style modern bluegrass band called the New Tradition. Not to be outdone, the powerful personality of John Duffey marched back into the picture.

Duffey joined with two key members of the Cliff Waldron band (dobroist Mike Auldridge and banjoist Ben Eldridge) and his old bassist from the Country Gentlemen days, the still youthful-looking Tom Gray, to form a new band. Guitarist John Starling was brought in to sing, and they called their band Seldom Scene.

To date, the Seldom Scene has recorded four LPs for the Washington-based Rebel label. They were hailed as some of the best ever recorded, and on the most recent they were joined by one of the most popular pop singers, Linda Ronstadt. It's too soon to tell, but the storm warnings are up, and the Seldom Scene may well be remembered as one of the most influential bands ever spawned in the ever-widening field of bluegrass music.

The *National Observer* recently called John Duffey the "father of modern bluegrass." He doesn't quite measure up to a "father" image in the Bill Monroe sense, but he certainly was there when it started. He was one of the big pushes behind the Country Gentlemen, who in turn were a big push behind the progressive bluegrass movement, which in turn will have an effect on the directions bluegrass might take tomorrow.

11

An Endless Festival

BRINGING IT OUT IN THE OPEN

To tens of thousands who follow bluegrass, summer means festivals. To some it's just a weekend away from everything, for others a chance to be a part of something big and exciting and sure to make the local headlines. A few of us go to most of them. Others can get away for only one or two a year. One thing is certain: Anyone who goes to one will go to another. One weekend at a good bluegrass festival can make a believer of anyone.

The days on the calendar have ambled by, and finally the big red circle marks our day of departure. The car is packed (with a minimum of swearing this year) and we've loaded the cooler chest, which houses our basic needs of bread, meat, and beer. Summer clothes have been packed in case it's hot, winter clothes in case it's cold, and the old Gibson mandolin laid gently in the case along with several Fender "heavy" picks and two sets of Gibson bronze-wound strings. If it's a good festival, we'll go through both sets.

It's off to Virginia. That old Stanley Brothers song keeps going through my head: "In the deep, rolling hills of old Virginia, there's a place I love so well. . . ." Carter was writing about the mountains, but that's not where we're headed. We're off to the flats of the Shenandoah Valley. The mountains don't usually have enough flat space to hold the thousands who attend these things. Even the big festival at Ralph Stanley's old home must have water trucked in from nearby Rose Hill, which, incidentally, is Earl Taylor's hometown. Yeah, the flat, rolling hills are a lot better. It's pretty hard to sleep in a tent pitched on a forty-five-degree slope.

AN ENDLESS FESTIVAL

Headlights flash by and the broken white line zings past on the left like machine gun bullets. The eight-track tape player is blaring and we're singing along with a tape I made last winter of some of the best of my old Red Allen records. She's singing tenor, I'm taking the baritone, and Red is singing the lead part. Not a bad trio (with the help of the Yates Brothers and the noise of the passing diesels) as we leave the Pennsylvania Turnpike and head down I-70 toward Hagerstown.

The road noise and the hypnotic sloshing of the beer cans in what's left of our ice causes my mind to wander a little. I'm a sixteen-year-old kid again, riding in a friend's car to our first job as a bluegrass band. It was at the grand opening of a Tastee-Freeze in Northridge, California. Actually, it was a talent contest, and we won first prize. There was a guy there who dressed like Lawrence of Arabia and played the bongos. Our stiffest competitors were two folk singers whose entire act was wiped out by the noise of a passing train on the track fifteen feet from the stage. One of the judges was the guy who played Tag on the "Annie Oakley" TV show, and a cop who loved bluegrass invited us to his house to meet his wife and tape some stuff on his tape recorder. We were delighted, and I got my first taste of performing and my first glimpse of the dedication and genuine kindness of the bluegrass devotee.

Then there was another time, not long after, when my grandmother encouraged us to enter a talent contest. First prize was an appearance on Cal Worthington's Sunday afternoon TV show on channel 13 in Los Angeles. The contest was held at a dive called the Foothill in the Long Beach oil fields, and we blew it. Another bluegrass band there, three older guys in hats and string ties, blew it, too. They called themselves the Blue Ridge Mountain Boys, which I thought was the greatest name in the world until I discovered there were about four thousand bands (even a couple in Japan, I think) with the same name. Anyway, we both lost the contest to a black dude who played the guitar like Chuck Berry and sang "I'm a Long, Tall Texan." It was a wasted night for everyone, because as far as I know, the black guy never made it to "Cal's Corral," and we had high school final exams the next day. Shortly after that our fourteen-year-old guitarist, Danny Levitt, was fired—by his mother.

My mind can really drift when I'm driving, and after hours of listening to my tapes and reliving the highlights of the Los Angeles bluegrass scene of the 1960s (including the day I rightfully decided that the East was where it was at), we're getting very close to our destination. Somewhere up the road is the turnoff I sleepily remember as the one we took last year. Yeah, there it is. A crude sign sticks lonesomely out of the ground over by the thistles and vetch. Its handwritten message, barely readable in the dark, simply says, in yellow-orange letters on an orange-yellow background: "FESTIVAL."

The road into the "park" is bumpy and dusty, even though it's quite late at night and the dew has settled heavily on the roadside grass. Those beer cans are really sloshing around now. There's a vague concern for the safety of the mandolin back there as we bump and jostle along, past pigpens, coon-dog pens, corncribs, and unpainted farmhouses. The moon is up—and the stars, too—and it's always a wonder to me that the people still live here with the earth in leaning three- and four-room farm shacks with chickens and washing machines on the front porches and junked cars and abandoned bathtubs in the front yards. And we're less than a half-mile from the interstate.

There are lights ahead. Strings of naked 200-watt light bulbs illuminate the ticket gate, obviously once the road gate of a cow pasture. The light bulbs provide only a thin disguise of the former function of these sixty acres of fertile Virginia farmland. It's late now, well past midnight, but two or three cars are still ahead of us in line, waiting for the ticket man to make change. Now it's our turn, and we pull up as our headlights bore through the dust from the car ahead of us.

The ticket man is fat and over forty. He wears a straw cowboy hat, soiled T-shirt, and needs a shave. In fact, he probably needed a shave yesterday and the day before that. There's a chew of tobacco the size of a duck's egg in his left cheek as he pokes his head in the car window (a little too close to my wife's face) and drawls, "How long y'all stayin?" We tell him and he takes our money and hands us two hospital-type plastic bracelets that we are warned must be worn at all times. He doesn't say what'll happen if we're caught without them, but from his look it will be something pretty terrible.

While he's fumbling for change, I glance over at the rainbow-hued poster wired to a shade tree. There's an old picture of Lester Flatt on it, probably taken at WPTF in 1951. Next to it is a picture of Mac Wiseman, taken almost as long ago, and there's a picture of the Osbornes in those sequined blue jackets they used to wear when they were really heavy. There are the characteristically ageless pictures of Bill Monroe and Jimmy Martin. The list of acts is at the bottom, and I realize only now that we drove all the way down here without the slightest knowledge of who would be playing. Del McCoury's name catches my eye, and the Country Gentlemen (shouldn't they have gotten their picture at the top, like the others?), and Ralph

Stanley's picture, off in the bottom corner. Way down at the bottom of the list are the new bands, the progressives, whose presence on the bill is supposed to bring in the rock-oriented people. The fact that the New Grass Revival was accorded last place on the bill tells me something of the tastes of the promoters.

The ticket man has finally found the correct number of nickels and dimes in the pocket of his dirty white carpenter's apron, and we start bumping our way out across the pasture. Here's a good sign: a jam session not more than ten yards from the ticket stand. I can always tell how good a festival is going to be from the amount of parking-lot music I can hear from the front gate. We slow down for a minute to see if they are any of our friends from other festivals. No, they have Oklahoma plates on their car. A tall, chin-whiskered, Abe Lincoln type is playing a guitar (not a Martin, from the sound of it) and singing that ever-popular Jimmy Martin tune, "Tennessee," while a very short guy with fuzzy hair hammers away at the banjo in the light of the opened trunk lid of a road-filthy Pontiac. A plastic trash bag hangs from one of the ornamental chrome things on the bumper; it's already half-full of empty beer cans, and the old boys are getting a little silly. They are joined by a girl of the "brown rice, brown flour, and knapsack" type lugging a bass. And from the other direction comes a guy carrying a mandolin, whom I remember from last year.

"Tennessee" continues, and they have a pretty good little band going until they come to the part where the bass singer is supposed to chime in with "I hear you callin' me," and they realize that they don't have a bass singer, and everything kind of disintegrates. Everyone laughs but the "knapsack" girl, who picks up her bass and disappears into the night. I thought it was funny, too, but it's time for us to vanish into the darkness in search of a piece of land flat enough to pitch a tent on.

Nothing, to me is more infuriating than having to go through the menial motions of setting up a camp at one o'clock in the morning while the night air is filled with the exquisite sound of bluegrass in the rough, the banjos and fiddles and high-tenor voices drifting out over the dew and fog like the ghosts of a forgotten mountain churchyard. My hands itch to get that mandolin and head off into the night looking for a hot session in need of a tenor-singing mandolin player. I feel like staying up all night and slamming that four-finger B chord and screaming the high harmony two or three keys above comfortable male vocal range.

But instead I pound tent pegs, pump up the pressure tank on the Coleman lantern, pump up the Coleman stove, blow up two air mattresses (by mouth—great for the tenor singing), and respond tersely in the negative when asked if I'm hungry, thirsty, or in need of something for my hay fever.

Everything's finished. It's time to make the rounds, to see who's here and what's going on out in the field. I've got the mandolin case and we're walking through the wet grass toward the sound of a bass fiddle booming somewhere over by a well-lit Winnebago.

It isn't the bass that catches my ear as we approach. Faces become clear in the light, and the sound of a beautifully played fiddle dances and twirls out of the buzz of voices and the meshwork of four or five instruments. The man with the bow, red-faced and balding, is one of those who make coming to these things worth the long drive, dust, heat, cold, and frequent cloudbursts. His name is Kenny Baker, and his presence in the field is one of the marks of a memorable festival.

We stand at the outskirts of the session with others drawn to the sweet, almost classical sound of Baker's fiddling. He prances fluidly through a number of old-time fiddle tunes—he knows hundreds of them—and polishes off one or two old jazz tunes at someone's request. A banjo player I don't recognize takes a break on the tune "Dry and Dusty" as Baker stops a moment to say hello to my wife and me. He's been a guest at our camp a few times.

Baker is a master, possibly the best bluegrass fiddler ever. He's been Bill Monroe's fiddler off and on since about 1956 and played on some of Bill's best stuff. He's been with Bill steadily now since 1967—he replaced Byron Berline when that young Oklahoma fiddler was drafted—and if Baker was well known before that, he has surely become a legend since. At the risk of sounding regionally prejudiced, I must say that it's hard for me to believe that the sublimely polished, Texas-style country-bluegrass-jazz fiddling we're listening to is being made by a former coal miner and part-time hog farmer from Jenkins, Kentucky. We tell Kenny to stop by our camp if he has a chance, he says thanks, he will, and we drift off to see if there's any other good music going on.

There is. The night is a little damp but beautiful. A light mist floats over everything, but straight up the moon and stars are bright and clear. There's a Canadian license plate, and as we pass we realize that none of the people in this camp are speaking English. A man is standing at the outskirts trying to tune a Baldwin banjo. He smiles up at us and says something to the effect that "It's hard to stay in tune when the air is so damp," but his accent is so thickly French that we can barely understand him. But we smile back in agreement, and I am again amazed at the variety of people who dig this stuff.

People come to these festivals from literally all over the world. One year at Monroe's festival at Bean Blossom, Indiana, Bill boasted from the stage that there were people present from every state—Alaska and Hawaii included—and five foreign countries. One of the bands booked that year was from New Zealand. People were amazed back in the late 1960s when Ralph Stanley toured one summer with a teen-aged mandolinist from England. Since then, it's become common. The Bluegrass 45 came over from Japan and proved they were better musicians with more of a feel for bluegrass than the majority of the young Americans playing. And there was the Blue Grass Connection from France a few years ago, and a friend of mine from Switzerland named Urs Von Arx who plays banjo and records with a band over there called the Country Ramblers. Monroe seems to take it all in stride, but I wonder what he really thinks of being the founder of a worldwide movement. I'm sure he didn't think much about it back in 1939 when he first yodeled the "Muleskinner Blues" into the WSM microphone.

No other stars in the field tonight, but then it's only Friday night. Anything can happen, but Saturday night's usually the hot one. I tell my wife about the time at Berryville when Red Smiley stopped over at the camp next to ours—right in back of my tent—and sang those old Reno and Smiley duets with someone until about two o'clock in the morning. And later, at Bean Blossom, when Reno and Smiley just stood in the dark and sang, leaning on a fence by the old jamboree barn with no more than three sleepy people standing there listening. Red had just rejoined Don and they were obviously savoring the reunion. Just a few months later Red was dead. It pays to try to be where it's happening, because some of what we'll hear this weekend will never be repeated.

As has been customary in recent years, the far end of the field is occupied by the younger people—hippies, if you will—and the music coming from that quarter is a bit less like the traditional sounds of Kenny Baker or Red Smiley. There are two people sitting on the wet grass, one playing a Yamaha guitar and the other playing some blues on a harmonica. We get a whiff of some grass and I feel a little uneasy thinking about the burly state policeman we just saw behind us. The one state trooper finding the one kid smoking grass could bring this festival and others to an end in this county, even though this is a "dry" county and most of the "straights" will be

127

drinking beer here all weekend. After Woodstock, the word *festival* took on an ugly meaning for a lot of righteous American taxpayers, and there's always the fear that a county commissioner will come in with a court order. That would be tragic, since the overwhelming majority of the festivals are the most relaxed and peaceful things imaginable. There are families here, elderly couples, college kids, and Carolina tobacco farmers, and things virtually never get out of hand. If there is trouble with the authorities, it's generally over something like not having enough water or portable toilets.

Ah, there are the buses, over on the other side of the main gate. These are the converted Greyhound and Trailways coaches that most of the bands drive these days, and there's often some very heavy jamming going on around or inside them, although only a select few are allowed within. I can read some of the names—Bill Monroe is one of them, tastefully lettered up in the little window box where the words *Detroit* or *St. Louis* once appeared. There's Flatt's bus, and the Country Gentlemen's, Ralph Stanley's—that's Curly Ray Cline silhouetted against the interior light. Then the light goes out—they're going to bed, and I guess we should, too. We've been up all day and we drove most of the night to get here, and my eyes feel grainy. A rooster is crowing somewhere.

The sleeping bag is warm, and now I'm glad I blew up the air mattresses while I was still a little fresh. But I can't get to sleep right away—I'm still too wound up and thinking. What is there about this music that makes me do this, that makes all of us do it? We drive all night, sometimes we drive for days, just to be near it, to sense its pulse. It's part of me and it was part of me from the first note of bluegrass I ever heard. I don't know what it did, what it said that made me love it instantly and with such intensity. I never really identified with my immediate ancestors in the mountains of northern Arkansas and the Pentecostal churches of Missouri, even though it might have had something to do with a grandmother who still calls skillets stewpots and has been going into bashful, blushing hysterics over Minnie Pearl's hat for over thirty years. I've bummed rides to festivals and slept unblanketed for three nights on the wet, hard ground and still felt at home and at peace. There's something about it that makes me feel that I really belong on the earth, that I have found something of myself in bluegrass.

And now, tonight, I can hear the thump of a bass, the bark of a mandolin, and the crackle of a banjo, with its fifth string pinging out over everything else. Then they stop and all that's left is one fiddle, way off in the other direction through the thickening fog. It must be a beginner caught up in the feel of the night, and he's playing the old breakdown "Katy Hill," but slow and ragged. No, maybe it's an old-timer, playing it the way he feels it tonight, slow and lonesome. Right now it sounds like the lonesomest thing in the world as it drones through the air, through the tent, through my head. Lying here with just the sound of that wailing and winding fiddle, I know that if I die before the sun comes up on this converted Virginia pasture, I will have died a contented and fulfilled man.

But the light of morning does come, and a little too soon, because I'm still dead tired and the sun is making the inside of this tent feel like a furnace. And my God, somebody's already up and playing music. Just outside I hear the pop and sizzle of bacon and smell coffee. My wife's already up and around, so what's the use? There are about three jam sessions going on, and I really wonder how people can just jump out of bed and start playing music. Well, I'm informed, it's hardly morning at all. It's almost eleven, and someone's up at the stage already, testing out the PA.

They're testing the sound system by playing a bluegrass record, one by a band called Jim Greer and the Mac-O-Chee Valley Folks. They aren't exactly a big name and I amaze my wife with the information, which she considers trivia. It's not—they're part of bluegrass and bluegrass is part of me, so what's trivial about it?

The program for today looks good. They don't usually bring on the really big guns until Sunday. We've eaten and washed and the mandolin is packed away in the car, out of sight. It's time to take our folding aluminum lawn chairs up to the stage area.

The stage is actually an unimpressive two-by-four-and-plywood structure with a small waiting room built onto the back for the performers. The stage is small and much of the view is blocked by a large speaker column at each corner. There is a swayback roof over it to keep sun and rain from dampening the spirits (and instruments) of the artists. The audience area is beautiful, with inviting oak and sycamore trees rustling in the first breezes of the Virginia morning.

Off to the sides and up from the seating area are two long wooden tables, one on each side, with cartons full of bluegrass records stacked on them. They sell bluegrass records here, and fans know they'd better buy them here because their record stores back home still don't know Bill Monroe from Vaughn Monroe. At one table is Dave Freeman of County records, with his wife and baby son. They're talking to a tall man wearing glasses and a cowboy hat, and I recognize him—Charlie Monroe, almost as legendary a figure in old-time country music and bluegrass as his younger brother Bill. On the other side is Freeman's competition, Ken Irwin of Rounder records, talking to one or two of the younger musicians.

People are starting to enter the stage area to find seats with good visibility before the mob moves in. Kids are playing around the stage, to the dismay of the sound technicians; there's a fat, corn-fed-looking woman dragging down one of those old-time wooden lawn chairs that they used to have on the decks of luxury liners; two young, bearded first-timers with frisky Irish setters are asking the sound technicians when the show starts. Soon the announcer appears, complete with cowboy boots and Sunday suit.

He's Jim Eanes, a good singer, one of the men who played with Monroe during that awkward period between Lester Flatt and Jimmy Martin, around 1950. He has had some great bands of his own, too, and a lot of his stuff is worth collecting. Unfortunately, Jim's voice fits more into the country crooner category than bluegrass, and there hasn't been much call for his style of singing in the past ten years or so. He'll be used primarily as an emcee this weekend, but he'll probably guest with some of the other bands and sing some of his old hits like "Your Old Stand-by," "I Wouldn't Change You If I Could," and "Little Old Log Cabin in the Lane".

"Smilin' Jim" rustles paper, clears his throat, loosens his Western tie. He exchanges on-mike pleasantries with the still-thin audience; "Didjall sleep okay?" "Sure glad it ain't raining," etc. The mike's too loud, the guy at the controls turns it down.

"Ladies and gentlemen, it's my great pleasure to introduce to you here today one of the pioneer acts of country music and bluegrass, one of the bands that kindly started a lot of us off. They've been away for a while, but we brought them back by public demand. So if I can have your undivided attention, join with me please and make welcome Bill and Earl Bolick, the Blue Sky Boys!"

The scattered patter of hands is slightly less than an ovation, and it seems to me a raw deal to put such an important act on before there is hardly an audience to hear them. Accompanied only by their own guitar and mandolin, they break into their old-time theme song, "Are You from Dixie?" a song that is more often associated with the later version by Grandpa Jones. It's one of the only up-tempo things they do, and they drift off into the soft duet singing that is, after all these years, still shattering in its simple beauty and directness.

I have to get closer to stage to get a good look at them. This is a first for me; I've never seen them live, and I've always admired their music. Another guy at the edge of the stage is staring as closely as I, and he turns to me halfway through their third number and says, "That's the most beautiful harmony in the world. There isn't a hot-shot bluegrass band at this festival who couldn't take a lesson from those two." I agree.

The audience grows as the show progresses. The Bolicks leave and are replaced by the hard bluegrass sound of Del McCoury. Del was probably Bill Monroe's finest "hard" bluegrass lead singer of the 1960s. He can sing high and strong and he's had a good band for a long time, but we can't help feel a little sadness in the fact that the growing world of bluegrass is outgrowing the straight, Monroe-style groups, of which McCoury's is one of the best.

Del leaves the audience with a driving version of one of the tunes he recorded with Bill, "Roll on, Buddy," and Jim Eanes announces Larry Sparks. Larry was just a kid when he crashed the bluegrass world in Ralph Stanley's band shortly after brother Carter Stanley died. He's still in his twenties and is one of the great hopes of the traditionalists. He's got it, whatever "it" is—presence, talent—and he's also got a hot band. All the musicians play and sing in a style most compatible to Sparks' neo-Stanley style. Larry is a superlative lead guitar player; not a lot of fast notes, but a touch that makes him more of an artist than nine-tenths of the flashy lead guitarists. The Sparks band is young and enthusiastic, and their enthusiasm is contagious enough to bring them back for an encore.

The still-growing crowd finally lets Sparks and his Lonesome Ramblers offstage, making way for one of the real pros, a silky-voiced South Carolinian named Charlie Moore. Eanes momentarily confuses the name of Moore's band, the Dixie Partners, with Del McCoury's Dixie Pals, but the differences are good-naturedly straightened out, and the balding, goateed Moore starts his patter with the audience in the smoothest, most pleasingly professional southern drawl anywhere. Moore recalls his days on King records with his old partner, Bill Napier, then sings his song about the "Rebel Soldier," which was recorded later by the Country Gentlemen and awarded *Muleskinner News*'s Song of the Year honors in the bluegrass field. Moore's style is soft and smooth, matching his resonant voice, but he gets the crowd going with a few numbers played in the old-time clawhammer style.

We haven't had enough of Charlie Moore, but his band makes their exit and the next band is announced and ushered on.

Perhaps *ushered* isn't the right word, because the band now on stage is Jimmy Martin and the Sunny Mountain Boys, and they are very sure of the way to the microphone. He's the last band on before the afternoon lunch break, and he really does a job. He talks and brags and tells jokes about his band members as though he were in a local tavern somewhere. Someone yells something to the effect that Jimmy should stop talking and start playing some music, but Jimmy is in full control and has a few snappy retorts. He starts off his set with the classic "Sunny Side of the Mountain," but there's a drunken local with his arm upon the stage trying to get Jimmy to sing it again. The old guy has a stubbled chin, dark-green work clothes, and one of those mesh-ventilated baseball fishing caps with the swordfish embroidered on the front, and Jimmy's banter with him is hilarious. But the audience is getting restless and a lot of people are wishing that Jimmy would stop messing with the old guy and get back to the music.

The audience isn't altogether saved when Jimmy asks his female bass player (complete with tight, sequined dress) to come up and sing one. Her name is Gloria Belle, she's from Pennsylvania Dutch country, and she's been taking Jimmy's on-stage insults since 1968. She breaks into a rousing song while Jimmy makes faces at her, holds his nose in a gesture of blunt criticism, and encourages the audience to boo, which it is too polite to do.

Gloria Belle, like most women bluegrass singers, leans toward that belt-'em-out Molly O'Day style. Molly was a legendary singer in the late 1940s who influenced many in her day, including the likes of country singers Rose Maddox and Wilma Lee Cooper. It's a good style, but the hard punchiness of bluegrass has yet to give rise to a superior female bluegrass singer. The ones who don't sound too soft and gentle often sound like hard-as-nails lady truck drivers. The women singers generally feel more comfortable with the new sounds of bluegrass, as do, for instance, Buck White's two daughters. I try to explain the situation to my wife, bringing up that fine Greenbriar Boys LP with Dian James singing lead, and I mention something about Linda Ronstadt, but now Gloria's song is over and Jimmy's back up at the mike. He announces his next tune, one of his latest MCA releases called "Fly Me to Frisco," and suddenly the band is offstage. The crowd wasn't with Jimmy today, but he'll probably make up for it tonight.

As the years have passed, I've found that my saturation point for the music on stage gets a little lower every year. Maybe it's because I can't listen to bluegrass very long without having to play it myself. Anyway, we've been bombarded with good music all morning and now it's time to walk around and see what's going on elsewhere. We leave the lawn chairs where they are—no one's going to walk off with them. Not at a bluegrass festival.

There's music blaring from every direction as we walk out of the shaded area and back into the sun, which is now quite high in the sky. Cars and campers have been pouring in by the hundreds while we've been sitting at the stage, and the field is full to the point of bursting as the dust flies and kids chase each other between the cars. A fat guy in T-shirt and cowboy hat (possibly last night's ticket man with a shave) waves cars into the empty parts of the field as they file into the grounds. There's hardly room left to squeeze them in; the place is literally crammed with cars and trucks, and there's a hot session going on at about every third car.

Trunk lids are open, beer coolers sit within easy reach, guitar and banjo cases are laid on the ground in the tiny pieces of shade under each car. Frantic banjo licks seem to come from everywhere. One session bleeds into the next for a clashing of sound that is confusing if not pleasing. "Roll in My Sweet Baby's Arms" jumps from a quartet of enthusiastic beginners; incredible variations of "John Hardy" leap from a bunch of very capable pickers just a few feet away. It's a good thing bluegrass isn't electric music; two electric bands couldn't get away with playing two different songs on opposite sides of the same VW bus.

License plates are from everywhere: California, Tennessee, Missouri, Michigan, Florida, Kansas, even one from New Mexico. Lots of them from Virginia, Maryland, and Pennsylvania. Sweating men squint in the sun, clasping capoed Martins, singing their versions of the songs of Bill Monroe and the Stanley Brothers. New waves can be detected in some of the newer songs that even the older guys are singing. A heavy guy with a canvas hat and ruddy, sunburnt face switches from the Stanleys' "Don't Step Over an Old Love" to a nice version of the Country Gentlemen's "Redwood Hill."

Now the action is really hot, and it will probably stay this way all night. Cars stream in, the fat guy with the cowboy hat is almost choking on the dust, and the music can be heard for miles. Farm couples with kids march toward the stage, duck-fashion, each carrying his own folding chair. Hawkers are walking through the crowd selling bluegrass T-shirts and bluegrass bumper stickers. A hugh brown canopy has been pitched across the little dirt cowpath in back of the stage, and the people under it are selling strings, banjo parts, songbooks, and all the other goodies that the bluegrass crowd might need during the weekend. That's Bucks County Music Store from up in Pennsylvania, and people are about four deep around their long, canopy-shaded tables.

There's music and dust and activity everywhere. Some guy's selling instruments from the trunk of his car. This is worth looking at. He's got a couple of old Martin D-28s, the big-bodied model treasured by bluegrass pickers everywhere. One's very dark on top, and he verifies my suspicion that it's from the late 1940s. The other one catches my eye, because the edges are inlaid with wood in a herringbone pattern. This is one of the classics, one of the rare ones made in the late 1930s, and their sound is great. He wants over a grand for it, and he'll probably get it, but not from me. I climb into the strap and run my thumb over the strings. Even without a pick, the husky resonance makes a passerby turn his head. The sound vibrations penetrate my body like a foot-massage machine, and I love it, but the price is too high. He's also got an old mandolin in the trunk that he isn't showing to most people. It's a Gibson F-5 model, the top of the line, made back in 1924 and signed by Gibson's legendary acoustical engineer, Lloyd Loar. Rumors are that these carved, inlaid, tastefully baroque beauties are worth a couple thousand and more. And all because Bill Monroe plays one.

Monroe bought his F-5 down in Florida in the 1940s, and today it looks like it's been tied to the back bumper of a car and dragged down a gravel road. But it has the sound that everyone who loves bluegrass has heard on all those classic Bill Monroe records, and that's the sound everyone wants from a mandolin. It's a loud, hoarse, throaty sound commonly described as "woody." My wife nudges me because she knows I have my own Loar now, bought before the market went up, locked right in the trunk of our car. And like Monroe's, mine is a 1923.

The music is all around us, and the look and sound of the guy's F-5 get me a little itchy to pick. But on the way back we are sidetracked by a crowd gathered around an old Chevy van. On the back bumper, between the opened tailgates, sits a handsome kid of about twenty with thick shocks of blond hair cascading to his shoulders. It's Sam Bush, of the New Grass Revival, and he's surrounded by about thirty people trying to keep track of the thousands of notes flying from his mandolin. Sam is one of the best instrumentalists around on mandolin and fiddle, and he's one of the young people bringing the sounds of rock into bluegrass. Some like it and some don't, but it's certain that the crowd around the skinny, blue-jeaned

Kentuckian is bigger than the crowd around anyone else out here in the field. It's interesting to note that rock superstar Leon Russell chose the "Revival" as the warmup act on one of his tours.

I'm making mental notes of the sessions around us, checking for the ones without mandolin players. Maybe I'll be welcome at one of them in a little while, once my mandolin is taken out of the trunk (where it's probably baking) and tuned up.

We've eaten lunch and some of our friends have pulled into the park, the people we like to camp with every year. They're all nice people and we like to pick with them and swap stories about our favorite bluegrass stars and some of the weird situations they get themselves into. There's a guy named Nick who plays the fiddle, and a tall guy named Pete from New York who can play guitar and sing bluegrass better than a lot of the country boys. And there's a banjo-playing airline pilot from Texas who likes to do an impression of Carter Stanley's recitation on "Whiskey and Jail" that is even funnier than the original.

Now's my chance to pick. This is what I've been waiting for since I've been here, and the moment is at hand. Pete, the guitar player, knows the songs and Nick and I know the choruses, and we've played together enough in the "field;" to know what the other guy's going to do, so it sounds at least halfway organized. People start to gather around. We've seen a lot of their faces at other festivals, and we nod and smile as we pick. We lay into a fast one, a tune Pete used to do while playing with Virginia mandolinist George Winn. I used to do the same number when I played with Mac Martin, so we don't have any trouble with it until a couple of guys start getting a little distracting by staring at my mandolin, their noses about an inch from my pick-hand, trying to read the paper label on the inside of the instrument. "Is that a 'Lloyd Loar'?" one of them asks. I have just enough time for a curt "yeah" from the side of my mouth, because it's time for my first mandolin break, and I want it to be good.

We've done about half a dozen songs and we think we've started to run out of material when the inevitable happens. An inebriated local comes stumbling through the crowd, a half-empty bottle of Miller's in his hand.

The locals are usually the bane of the avid festival-goer. They come out of curiosity and they don't really know why they're here—most of them don't know how to drink and get roaring drunk on a few bottles of beer and go around getting into trouble. It's a carnival to them, an excuse to go out and get themselves ripped. After all, they'll never see any of these people again, and if there's any real trouble—like if someone decides to lay a beer bottle across someone's head—it's the festival people who'll take the blame.

So this guy shows a general ignorance of bluegrass by asking us to play a song we all know but can't stand. We lie a little and tell him that we don't know it, but he starts singing it anyway, very loudly, and several members of our little audience drift off, not wanting to witness the ruination of a good jam session. Somehow, we think of a song we all know that's better than the one the drunk is singing, and we lay into it like thunder, hoping the drunk won't know it, will feel stupid, and will vanish.

We were right on one count: The drunk doesn't know the song. But that doesn't stop him from singing it with us. The last vestiges of our once-enthusiastic audience have given up and moved on. We'll laugh about this tomorrow, but for now we figure it's time for a breather.

The sun is really hot now, and it's a good thing we brought our own shade, the big canvas canopy that has served us for many outings. Things are quiet now, almost as quiet as when we pulled in last night. Everybody's eating lunch. We have a chance to sit back now, eat a sandwich, and look around us. This is where bluegrass belongs. It's flat where we are now, but there are mountains all around us, and the air is as clear and as free from haze as the deserts I used to know in California. There's a song that keeps going through my head now, a song by the Louvin Brothers that I have on a record at home. It's called "Alabama," the Louvins' salute to the place they knew as boys. Its words look pretty corny on paper, but they say the same things John Denver sang of in his "Country Road." Ira and Charlie Louvin have lived it, and it shows in their writing. When they sing you can almost see the images, the red leaves in autumn with 'possums crawling in the furrows between dried cornstalks and the caged blue-tick hounds whining and barking because the chill in the air tells them it's time for the hunt. They sing of laboring in the sorghum mill and the childhood impressions of creeks, singing with laughter and roaming through pastures with "fences of rail."

That's what I see and hear now, looking above the car tops at the low hills that flank the "Vale of Shenandoah," which the Carter Family sang of so long ago. This is where bluegrass belongs, out here in the sunlight, not hidden in the back dressing rooms at the "Grand Ole Opry," not in the dingy gin mills of Columbus. Exposed to the air and sun, it can grow, and others can see how it's growing. Bluegrass stands in the music world as a breath of fresh air, and it's being discovered as such by thousands of the same jaded palates who are discovering that cold, sweet, deep-rock spring water is God's gift to thirst. The rippling banjo sounds so much better out here than anywhere else, and I could spend the rest of my life here.

This scene is nothing new, as much as some festival enthusiasts would like to think otherwise. There are decided similarities between the bluegrass festival and the old-time fiddlers' conventions, and surely the old-time revival camp meetings my dad used to tell me about, where all weekend they would sing, preach, camp, and eat picnic-style.

People have been getting together in the country to make music for many years. Back in the days when all music was local and each area had its own popular fiddler, they would get together once a year and have a convention. For those of a competitive nature, there were contests to see who was the best, and they developed special showy licks that were sure to win the judges' attention and admiration. Sometimes the convention was held in conjunction with another event, like a Confederate soldiers' reunion or some of the larger family reunions, which were almost like the old Scottish clan gatherings.

The fiddlers would do their stuff and play their best tunes, and the one who made the best impression (or slipped the right official a jug of something homemade and potent) would walk away with a little prize money and a ludicrously overblown title such as World's Champion Fiddler or National Fiddling Champion. There's no telling how many old-time fiddlers walked away from these contests believing they'd been judged the best fiddler on the planet Earth.

Fiddlers John Carson of Georgia and Eck Robertson of Texas were "discovered" at such conventions and subsequently became two of the earliest commercially recorded country musicians. A lot of other old-time greats made the contest rounds, too, and men like "Fiddlin'" Arthur Smith and Clayton "Pappy" McMichen were generally always contest winners in their prime. Prizes would be given for the best guitarist and the best string band, and the contests were often held as fund-raisers for schools or other organizations. Such was the case of the old-time fiddlers' convention at Union Grove, North Carolina.

The Van Hoy family has been associated with the Union Grove convention since it was first held over a half-century ago. Since the 1920s the little mountain school had opened its grounds to fiddlers, banjo pickers, clog dancers, and old-time string bands over the Easter weekends. The contest was held under a big top, and the event had become an institution for thousands. Therein lay a problem.

Easter weekends are not well thought of by many resort owners. For years, places like Florida's Fort Lauderdale and California's Balboa Island have received negative press attention because of the raucous young people who crowd the streets. The pressures of school have been great, the students have been cooped up all winter, and now the weather's nice and they want to get out and do something. They don't especially care where they're going or what they're going to do; they just have a lot of pent-up energy to burn off. Increasing thousands have been burning it off in the otherwise quiet little area around Union Grove. Motorcycle gangs are reported, thousands of half-clad long-hairs outrage the local populace, girls with papoose-style kids boogie in the aisles under the old big top while the management fights to keep electric instruments off the stage. Property has supposedly been destroyed, and national headlines have appeared saying, "HIPPIES IN-VADE HILLBILLY WOODSTOCK."

It's unfair to the thousands who attend with a genuine interest in what's going on up on the stage. But the loyalists began staying away, because for them it was becoming a nightmare. The school closed its gates to a scene that was getting out of hand, and the Van Hoys had to take their convention elsewhere.

Like most of the old-time fiddlers' conventions, the bluegrass festivals started small. Unlike the conventions, they are of a very recent vintage. The first festival was held in the summer of 1965 at Fincastle, Virginia, near Roanoke. Carlton Haney, promoter and once manager of the Reno and Smiley team, was the mastermind. He saw that bluegrass was just on the verge of beginning to break and that if the thousands of underground bluegrass fans knew they could go to one park on one weekend and see all the bluegrass stars whom they had been forced to admire almost secretly, they would probably come from the ends of the earth.

He wasn't far from wrong, although the idea took a few years to catch on. I missed the first one—I heard about it after the fact—and plans were being made to attend the second one when I was drafted. The crowd wasn't overwhelming the first year although nearly every name in the business was there. But within two years the crowds numbered into the thousands.

The festivals have had a huge effect on the style and sound of bluegrass. Between 1945 and 1965 bluegrass was a hard commodity to come by. You had to know where to look on the radio dial, and even then the most devout fans could go for months without being able to hear any bluegrass at all. Records were bought and played until every note was memorized and daylight was showing between the worn-out grooves. Bands could go for months—or even years—hearing very little of their competition, and with the exception of some of the groups that were groping into other markets by changing their sounds or plugging in, bluegrass was at pretty much of an artistic standstill by the early 1960s. With the birth of the festivals, bands were forced into change. They had to give the audience something new every year, and something a little different from what the other bands were giving them. They had to come up with new material, too, and many stars found that they had to look for the new material in some unusual places. The bluegrass fan was no longer starved for music, would no longer go bananas over the old chestnuts like "Love, Please Come Home" or "Will You Be Lovin' Another Man?"

So now there are hundreds of festivals—big ones and little ones—and some of the stars run their own, which eliminates the middleman and puts the money into the hand in which it belongs. Some of the big ones have drawn more than ten thousand people, and the music is going through good and bad changes because of them.

The festival we are attending, for example, is a good one. There is no trouble, everyone comes because there is bluegrass here, and they know what it is and love it. There is a feeling of genuine brotherhood. I just saw a kid with hair halfway down his back playing banjo with four rural types in their mid-forties who might have done the kid some physical damage if he'd walked into a southern truck stop and tried to make time with one of the waitresses. But they were smiling all around, having a good time, getting to know one another, and playing the same music. The rural types are flattered that a well-educated kid from the North loved "their" music so much that he got that good on the banjo. In turn, he's flattered because they let him play with them. When the kid left, one of the guys called after him, "Y'all come back after lunch, now. Our fiddle player should be here by then."

Still, other festivals are having their problems. There are people there who shouldn't be at a bluegrass festival, and an awful lot of them sneak in without paying. They don't know. They think they're doing something really slick by getting something for nothing. They don't realize the years of anguish behind bluegrass or how many years the performers spent starving on the road before the festivals hit. It's the same as ten years ago, when I was letting all my friends tape my bluegrass records before a friend of mine, banjoist Dave Magram, told me why I shouldn't. Bluegrass records are small sellers, and every time I let someone tape a record, I'm taking a few cents of royalty money out of someone's pocket. Every time I sneak a friend into a bluegrass festival, I am taking money out of Don Reno's pocket, or Bill Monroe's, or Ralph Stanley's. These are the great, unsung giants of American music, men who have paid their dues ten times over, who are only now beginning to claim some reward.

People just don't know. They think that bluegrass is something camp and fun and a good way to spend a weekend. At the festival at Gettysburg, the nonpaying guests poured across the river like cattle crossing the Rio Grande while the paying guests sat in their camps and watched. And it's the gate-crashers who get up in front of the stage and boogie while Bill Monroe sings a gospel tune.

As the festivals grow and the big ones get a little more out of hand each year, we can't help wondering where it's all going to end. Hopefully, it won't get to be like Union Grove, choking to death on motorcycle fumes. Tonight we'll go back up to the stage and listen to Monroe and Lester Flatt and the Osbornes and the New Grass Revival and the Seldom Scene. Tomorrow it will be the Lewis Family and the Country Gentlemen, and on through the afternoon show, where Bill gets up and sings with his old sidemen. There'll be duets with Clyde Moody, Jim Eanes, Carl Story, Flatt, Martin, Wiseman, and a trio or two with the Osborne Brothers. Then we'll head for home—limp, tired, happy, and temporarily satiated.

12

Up to Date
and Down to Earth

Some would have you believe that the bluegrass boom is nothing new. Those involved in it have been called revivalists, which isn't accurate. Bluegrass is not being revived—it is at the height of its popularity right now. The closest bluegrass had ever been to mass acceptance was in the early 1950s, when it just wasn't *that* different from the "straight" country music being pushed. If any popular country acts of 1952 had carried a Scruggs-style banjo picker, they would have been considered bluegrass. But they didn't, and they weren't.

There are dozens of labels now, large and small, recording scores of high-grade bluegrass bands. Ten years ago it was possible for a fan to own a copy of every bluegrass LP ever made and still have room on the shelf for a bust of Nefertiti or Franz Liszt. Today that same fan still could probably own all the records, but he'd have to rent a neighbor's garage to keep them in.

Twelve years ago I subscribed to *Sing-Out!* the voice of the folk music set, because once or twice a year they made reference to bluegrass. Now there are three major magazines devoted to bluegrass (possibly more that I haven't heard of), and they are a healthy part of the bonanza that the long-timers are finally able to bask in. There's Washington's *Bluegrass Unlimited*, Haney and Bartenstein's *Muleskinner News*, and now there's a new one called *Pickin'*, which is by far the most professional. I recently saw copies of *Pickin'* for sale at one of those superstraight, Hammon organ-oriented music stores in a huge suburban shopping mall. Now, I consider *that* an accomplishment: a monthly bluegrass mag being pushed on the same display rack with *Mel Bay's 1,000 Chords for the Hawaiian Guitar* and *The Self-Taught Saxophonist.*

I spent almost seven years with a bluegrass band playing bars in Pittsburgh, and I witnessed an amazing thing: the faces in the crowd. From what I could see through the dim lights and thick smoke, the usual faces at the beginning of those seven years were those of middle-aged workingmen and their wives. Many were from West Virginia, but there was a smattering of the well-educated who had been coming down to hear bluegrass since the folk music days.

Then the faces started to change; they started getting younger. By 1970 the young and old were there in equal number. Two years later the young outnumbered the old.

There is something very gratifying in that. In these days, when youth is worshiped, a healthy percentage of that youth is worshiping bluegrass. That is especially gratifying to me, a native of California who was thought strange by the surfboard set because I had a grainy picture of Bill Monroe, not the Beach Boys, on my bedroom wall. Now kids younger than I was then are coming to me with their Japanese banjos frantically seeking instruction because their high school pals are starting a bluegrass band and they don't want to be left out.

The numbers and kinds of people in bluegrass are surprising. I couldn't believe it when "blackgrass" (a mixture of soul and banjo that subsequently fizzled) hit the scene. And I'll never forget the night a black kid carrying a banjo case came in to the bar where we were playing. The guys I was playing with were in their thirties and forties and not exactly college liberal types. But the kid started a conversation with our fiddler, a fine musician named Mike Carson. Mike picked up his fiddle and the youngster took out his banjo, and they started playing a couple of the old things like "Old Leather Britches," "Soldier's Joy," and "Sugar in the Gourd." When I left to go home, they were still playing.

Still, with all its diversity, bluegrass has yet to reach the firm-footed status that folk music enjoyed fifteen years ago. It's interesting to follow the lineage of pop-folk music, and it's always been my opinion that the folk groups were a followup of the Calypso movement of Harry Belafonte, Trinidad, and the banana boats. When an enthusiastic trio from California recorded a song about "Tom Dooley," they used a conga drum and took their name from the town of Kingston, Jamaica. They broke the folk-pop

The Dillards. This fine Missouri-born group crashed the gates of bluegrass in the early 1960s with their appearances on the "Andy Griffith Show." In the mid-1960s they followed their fortune into the field of folk-bluegrass-rock. Seated on fence are Herb Pederson and Mitch Jayne. Kneeling in foreground are Rodney Dillard and Dean Webb.

The Shenandoah Cut-Ups, lined up and ready to step onto the festival stage. From left to right, they are Billy Edwards, Herschel Sizemore, John Palmer, Tater Tate, and Wes Golding. With the exception of Golding, the Cut-Ups are solid veterans who have played with many of the great names in bluegrass. Sizemore and Golding have recently been replaced by guitarist Udell McPeak and mandolinist Gene Burrows, who, along with Tate, Edwards, and Palmer, were Red Smiley's band through the late 1960s. (*Paul Gerry/Revonah Records*)

The Allen Brothers, sons of legendary bluegrass singer Red Allen, bring the appearance and ideas of today to the sound they absorbed from their father's music. Pictured are Neal, Greg, and Harley. A fourth brother, Ronnie, plays electric bass and drums. Neal, a highly talented singer, mandolinist, and songwriter, died suddenly of pneumonia in 1973. He was twenty-two years old. (*Barbara Batterton*)

John Hartford, a talented Missourian who lapsed from straight bluegrass to a soft, personal style that is decidedly out of the mainstream. Glen Campbell's recording of Hartford's "Gentle on My Mind" and John's subsequent appearances on the Campbell show did much for his career and for mass acceptance of bluegrass. (*Ron Petronko*/ Bluegrass Unlimited)

The New Grass Revival. Courtney Johnson, Sam Bush, Ebo Walker, and Cur Burch bring the look and sound of rock bluegrass. (*Barbara Batterton*)

The Country Gentlemen has provided a springboard for other bands, each changing and elaborating upon the sound much the same as the early Blue Grass Boys did when they left Bill Monroe. The Seldom Scene is an example. Two of its members were formerly with the Gentlemen. Left to right: John Starling, Ben Eldridge, Mike Auldridge, Tom Gray, and John Duffey. (*Carl Fleischhauer*/Bluegrass Unlimited)

Jimmy Gaudreau, the young mandolinist who replaced John Duffey with the Country Gentlemen, is seen here with his own group, the Country Store. It's probably unfair to call this band a spin-off from the Gentlemen, but Gaudreau does owe stylistic debts to the Gentlemen sound and to John Duffey in particular. They are exponents of the Washington sound. Left to right: Bill Rawlings, Dick Smith, Jimmy Gaudreau, and Chris Stifel.

Three generations of banjoists, mandolinists, and fiddlers gather around for a festival jam session at the Carter Stanley Memorial Festival at McClure, Virginia. The center of attraction here is legendary mountain musician Tommy Jarrell, playing the fiddle. (*Karen Artis*)

Parking lot jam sessions may include the rankest amateurs or the biggest stars. The principals at this session are two of Monroe's Blue Grass Boys, Joe Stuart and Kenny Baker. Stuart has been with Monroe off and on for over twenty years, playing almost every instrument. Baker is recognized as probably the greatest living bluegrass fiddler. (*Karen Artis*)

The Blue Grass Boys quartet in the early 1970s. One of the most popular aspects of Monroe's music has been in the field of gospel quartet singing. Here, at a Sunday morning festival "gospel sing," Monroe is joined by Jack Hicks (Bill's immediate right) and veterans Monroe Fields and Joe Stuart. (*Karen Artis*)

Bill Monroe and the Blue Grass Boys in the 1960s. Monroe's power to draw the best young musicians into his music hasn't waned over the years. Pictured here are four of the best. Left to right: Monroe, fiddler Byron Berline, banjoist Lamar Grier, bassist James Monroe, and guitarist Roland White. James is Bill's son and now heads his own band, the Midnight Ramblers. Berline and White are now members of the Country Gazette, one of the most popular of the new bands. Grier still plays around his native Baltimore after having recorded some of Bill's best work of the late 1960s. (*Erik Shank*)

South Carolinian Charlie Moore has been a mainstay in the field for many years. Much of his international reputation comes from the fine records he made for King with his former partner, Bill Napier. (*Tom Henderson*)

"Little" Roy Lewis stops the show by sneaking on stage and doing a riotously accurate impression of Ralph Stanley—and even steals Ralph's hat. One of the moments that makes hanging around the stage worthwhile. (*Karen Artis*)

Festival finales usually involve all of the stars getting together and doing a set, which may be fantastic or chaotic. From left: Curly Ray Cline, Kenny Baker, Ricky Skaggs, Jack Hicks, Leslie Keith, Bill Monroe, Bill Harrell (partially hidden), Ralph Stanley, Jimmy Martin, Charlie Waller, Kentucky Slim, Melvin Goins, the late Roy Lee Centers, Jack Cooke, and Joe Stuart. (*Karen Artis*)

Bill Monroe and Doc Watson often team up to re-create the sounds of the Monroe Brothers. This occasion was not a happy one; it was the Carter Stanley Memorial Concert, held in Washington, D.C., in the spring of 1967. (*Paul Gerry*)

barrier, and a revival and revolution were underway. It begat a renewed awareness of balladeers like the late Woody Guthrie, which begat Bob Dylan, which begat folk-rock, which begat country rock. And somewhere in the background, there was always bluegrass, waiting to surface. Surface it has, because now we're in the middle of a little revolution of our own.

Or maybe we're just a link in the chain of musical evolution, waiting to materialize into some new and surprising form. We do know there are some very interesting things going on within the ranks of bluegrass that are leading us well out of the old style and into something new, almost like swing music led to bebop twenty-five years ago.

We buy bluegrass records today, and it's not unusual to hear the songs of Gordon Lightfoot, James Taylor, or Tanya Tucker played on the banjos and mandolins, the fiddles and dobros, with good, solid, bluegrass trios. And it's nothing new anymore to see a full drum set and electrically amplified instruments on the stages of the bluegrass festivals. The old-timers shake their heads, the new-timers consider the artistic possibilities, and those of us in the middle are wisely going to wait a few years before voicing an opinion.

Long hair and short hair, drums and cymbals. The older people filter away from the stage as the New Grass Revival breaks into a rocking rendition of Leon Russell's "Prince of Peace" with Sam Bush singing like it's the Earth's last day and Courtney Johnson taking five-minute ad lib banjo breaks that nearly exhaust the mathematical possibilities of the three-octave modal-chromatic runs.

Then the older people filter back and the young wander off when the Shenandoah Cut-Ups come on for an hour of old-time bluegrass, the way it used to be played, with Billy Edwards laying out the straight, hard Scruggs-style with an enthusiasm that many have lost and some never achieve. It's sad that there's hardly a place on the same stage for these two very different styles that most people still put under the single heading of bluegrass.

Rock and bluegrass have been converging for the past few years. Chris Hillman, once a San Diego mandolin picker before becoming one of the original Byrds, never completely broke away from the stuff. We used to see him every Saturday night on television with a band called the Blue Diamond Boys (also called the Hillmen). They were a little unorthodox even then, back before the Byrds, doing bluegrass versions of the Dylan songs. We thought we'd lost him until we heard that "Last of the Flying Burrito Brothers" LP, wherein he and Byron Berline, Roger Bush, and some other fine bluegrass men laid down some hard stuff that drove their live rock audience wild.

Hillman's association with the Byrds came as a shock to a lot of us, but it eased the shocks to come, such as SeaTrain, the country rock band that includes two of Bill Monroe's best sidemen of the 1960s, fiddler Richard Green and singer Pete Rowan. A surprise we weren't prepared for, however, was Leon Russell's version of "Roll in My Sweet Baby's Arms."

The Nitty Gritty Dirt Band straddles a musical fence, playing commercial music while obviously having personal artistic leanings toward the music on their "Will the Circle Be Unbroken?" album, which should be enshrined. John Hartford and Earl Scruggs and his three sons straddle that same fence, while fiddler Vassar Clements is known almost as well today as a rock session man as he has been as a bluegrass sideman for the past twenty-five years. And no one can deny that people like Gram Parsons, Jerry Garcia, Seals and Crofts, Douglas and Rodney Dillard, and even Byron Berline and his Country Gazette are bridging the gap between rock and country styles that more and more are crossing—from both directions.

Nashville must have been surprised to find everyone else jumping on the bluegrass wagon. When it finally did sink in, the movement was well underway, and "Music City" wasn't quite sure how it had happened. Flatt and Scruggs had to go to Hollywood to make their only two national hits, one the theme for a TV show and the other theme music for a movie. Before the *Deliverance* rage broke, someone at the Country Music Association decided that they'd better get with it, and Bill Monroe's face was stamped on a bronze plaque and hung in their hall of fame.

It was indeed an honor long overdue, but there were many who looked at the whole thing with suspicion. Why, after ten years of ignoring bluegrass, had Nashville softened? Possibly because there was money to be made from it. Certainly the money that was made on bluegrass wasn't made by the performers, even though Monroe's earning power was probably increased by the hall of fame award.

Bluegrass fans were heartened when announcements came from the Tennessee capital that the move was on for bluegrass. Nothing much has come of it, except that a bluegrass concert is usually featured at the big country DJ's convention (one of country music's most important early events—a week of concerts and shoptalk in Nashville for all country DJs). The only bluegrass we've heard on our local country top-forty station was from the bluegrass albums of two nonbluegrass singers, Buck Owens and

144

Carl Smith. I could hardly suppress a low groan when someone came up to me in a bar where I was playing and asked me for "one of those Buck Owens tunes, like 'Ruby' or 'Roll in My Sweet Baby's Arms.'"

Change begets change, and the nudges and prods from the worlds of rock and country have made bluegrass a little more conscious of itself. The youth image has made its mark even in some of the oldest, most established bands. A torch has been passed, for example, in Lester Flatt's group. A sixteen-year-old Mississippian with Donny Osmond looks named Marty Stuart has been playing some remarkable mandolin with Flatt's Nashville Grass, leaving Curly Sechler (Flatt's off-and-on mandolinist since 1949) to sit back and chord the guitar. Curly, never an ace instrumentalist, tells the audience jokingly that he "taught Marty everything he knows."

Some are going forward into new things, others are stepping back to some of the older concepts. Red Allen, once a bastion of traditionalism, now performs a version of rock's "Proud Mary" with his sons Harley, Ronnie, and Greg. His former song-mates, the Osborne Brothers, have recently been seen playing their old, nonelectric instruments on stage. Allen realized the bluegrass world couldn't survive another year on a diet of "Salty Dog" and "Foggy Mountain Breakdown" at about the same time the Osbornes realized that a big part of the switch to bluegrass was getting back to the strengths of yesterday.

The old and the new. Traditionalism and newgrass are heading off in two different directions, and the bluegrass sound will probably reach an artistic end somewhere in the middle. Promoters book different festivals, one for newgrass, one for the old, and everyone's waiting to see what's going to happen next. There's a future, but what form will it take?

The Stanley Brothers' old records are still listened to, but even the staunchest supporters of the old style admit that Jimmy Gaudreau can probably outpick anyone who was playing the mandolin fifteen years ago, including (blasphemy!) Mr. Monroe himself. It would be very comforting to think that this great music, in ten years, will have reached that blessed middle-point, an easy sound that lies somewhere between the Goins Brothers and the Earl Scruggs Review, or between Carl Story and the New Grass Revival. In the struggle to either make the two compatible or sever the ties completely, someone is going to come along. Someone who can play the banjo or guitar or mandolin with the technical skill of a Horowitz or a Casals and who has the guts and soul of all the Stanleys and Monroes put together. Some say it's Larry Sparks, others say it's Ricky Skaggs, and some have said the Rice Brothers are already doing it with J. D. Crowe's band in Kentucky. A hillbilly Messiah? Why not? It's fairly obvious that someone will have to carry the torch when Bill Monroe is gone. And hasn't Monroe occupied such a position for over thirty years.?

Monroe is a vibrantly healthy man who probably has another twenty years of active life. But what happens when he goes? It's been pointed out many times that his presence keeps a lot of bands playing it straight. They respect the man to a point where what he thinks of them *means* something to them. George Hay, founder of the "Opry," is often cited for his stern, finger-shaking "Keep it down to earth, boys." Since his death the "Opry" and country music have turned away. Hopefully, when Bill Monroe is gone, there will be someone who will "keep it down to earth" while keeping its head and ears in the present. Bluegrass realizes it will die unless it keeps pace with the rest of the music world. It must also accept the fact that the Studebaker Company didn't save the horse and buggy by going into the automobile business. Modern country music changed and modernized itself to a point where it lost its soul and identity. Bluegrass deserves a better fate.

But the lesson of bluegrass goes beyond the lessons of country music, beyond the glories of acceptance by most of the other music styles as a valid member of the single world of music.

It's a lesson of people who wouldn't let die something they knew was great and good, even if they couldn't tell you why. It's a lesson of survival, of tenacity, of great men and their music who wouldn't let their love of comfort steer them away from a path they knew was right. They just couldn't deny the gooseflesh that appeared on their forearms when the Stanley Brothers sang "Lonesome River" or the excitement they felt the first time they heard "Foggy Mountain Breakdown" on a pop-country station.

There has to be something that makes people stand all night in the ankle-deep mud of a festival parking lot singing until they're hoarse and picking until their fingertips are blistered. And there has to be something in the music to make a small crowd shiver in the rain at Pennsylvania's Idlewild Park, waiting for the announced appearance of Red Smiley. It's the same something that made a thin, emaciated Smiley stand in the same rain and play for them. People made bluegrass, and people who loved and cherished it kept it from meeting the fate it could very easily have met in the mid-1950s. The bluegrass movement is a grass-roots movement that came only from the people. Therein lies its greatness, its greatest strength, and the reason we'll be hearing it for many years.

Appendix

RECORDINGS, PUBLICATIONS, RADIO STATIONS, ORGANIZATIONS

RECORDINGS

Buying bluegrass records has always been a risky proposition. How many times has the unwary buyer brought home a Jim and Jesse or Mac Wiseman to find that none of it was bluegrass? Some artists have confused the issue by recording the same songs twice, once in bluegrass style and once with straight country backup. If you can find any of the following records at your local record outlet, buy them. If you spot a record by someone whose name you recognize from this book but are unsure as to its content and are unable to listen to it before you purchase it, buy it anyway. It might be a good one; if it isn't, you will have learned something that will make you a more wary bluegrass record buyer.

Something that must be kept in mind while buying records: If you spot it, *buy it*. I must have passed over the Osborne Brothers' "Country Pickin' and Hillside Singin'" a hundred times, always promising myself that I'd come back next week and buy it. I came back, but by then it was gone. It has since become something impossible to get without paying a collector's price for. What looks like a major label release today may be in the collector's category next year.

And don't ever pass a "cheapie" record or tape bin at the local super-market or discount store without looking it over. I've found some prized records there, including Capitol's "Rose Maddox Sings Bluegrass" (wherein she is accompanied by Reno, Smiley, and Bill Monroe), the Country

Gentlemen's "Bluegrass at Carnegie Hall," "Country Pickin' and Hillside Singin'," and the great stuff the Osborne Brothers recorded in the early 1950s under the name Stanley Alpine. The "cheapie" bins almost always carry things that are no longer in the catalogs, and usually at a price that is only a fraction of what you pay for a new release.

One policy I've adopted over the years is that of buying records straight from the artist. Most of them sell records at their personal appearances, and I get more pleasure from seeing Tater Tate slip my five dollars into his wallet than when I shell out the same five to a record store.

It would be overly ambitious of me to list every bluegrass record ever made in this brief appendix, or even to list all the recordings of the major bands. But what I'm giving you here should be a more than adequate sampling of some of the best.

Bill Monroe

No collection of bluegrass recordings can call itself complete without a healthy sampling of Bill Monroe. To be frank, not everyone in bluegrass likes his music, especially those drawn to the smoother sounds. Bill's voice and playing can be harsh as he pushes his tenor up into the high registers. He is the embodiment of the "soul" aspects of bluegrass, and as such, his music is often rugged, raw, and intense.

I've always felt that there were five Monroe "periods": the Monroe Brothers; the early Blue Grass Boys on Victor; the early Columbia band (1945); the "classic" Columbia band (1946-1949); and the Decca period. Unfortunately, there has never been a Monroe Brothers album released in the United States, only in Japan. There was one devoted to the music of Bill and Charlie, but the contents were actually a mixture of the Monroe Brothers and the later work of Charlie Monroe—which was excellent and important. That material was released on the RCA Camden label, as was "The Father of Blue Grass," an excellent collection of the first recordings made by Bill and his band in 1940-1941. This album, which includes the work of Clyde Moody and Tommy Magness, includes the very important cuts of "Muleskinner Blues" and "In The Pines," as well as other very fine material from Monroe's first years at the "Opry." There are also two early Blue Grass Boys cuts, gospel quartets, on the RCA "Vintage" anthology "Early Bluegrass."

APPENDIX

The Monroe Columbia material has been well represented on three albums, which seem to be in and out of print with some regularity. "The Great Bill Monroe" (HL 7290), "Bill Monroe's Best" (HL 7315), and "The Original Bluegrass Sound" (HL 7338) have all been released on Columbia's Harmony sublabel. The first two are mixtures of the early Columbia bands (complete with accordion) and the "classic" group with Flatt, Scruggs, Chubby Wise, and Cedric Rainwater. The third in the series is devoted entirely to that great band, the one that literally *made* bluegrass. It is one of the essential albums in any bluegrass collection.

Monroe and his band have recorded a tremendous amount of material for Decca (now MCA) since 1950, too many albums to mention here. Not all of it is great, but it's all solid bluegrass and worth owning. Three of the most important albums are reissues, beautifully annotated by the Smithsonian's Ralph Rinzler, and these are perhaps the pick of the best Decca material. One is titled "Bluegrass Instrumentals" (DL 4601) and includes some powerful fiddling and mandolin playing and a good deal of insight into Monroe's instrumental genius. A second LP, "The High, Lonesome Sound" (DL 4780), spotlights the bluesy, mournful aspects of the Blue Grass Boys sound, with outstanding performances by Bill, Jimmy Martin, Carter Stanley, Sonny Osborne, and some of his best fiddlers. The third collection is devoted to Monroe's gospel sound: "A Voice From on High" (DL 75135) is possibly the finest all-gospel bluegrass album ever released, featuring many of the performers mentioned above.

Lester Flatt and Earl Scruggs

Flatt and Scruggs and their band have recorded on their own since 1948, and their early material on the Mercury label, some of the finest ever recorded, seems always to be in print in one form or another. The original cuts of "Foggy Mountain Breakdown," "Roll in My Sweet Baby's Arms," "Salty Dog Blues," and others have been issued, reissued, and reissued again since *Bonnie and Clyde* made "Foggy Mountain" into such a tremendous hit in the late 1960s. This material may be found almost everywhere on the Mercury, Mercury–Wing, and Pickwick/33 labels. Some of it has been overechoed and poorly rechanneled, but it's worth owning because the greatness of the music overshadows any technical botching.

Lester and Earl joined Columbia just as Monroe was leaving it. The

149

problem in buying the Columbia material is that Flatt and Scruggs changed so much between 1950 and 1969. The classics are "Foggy Mountain Jamboree," long out of print, and "Foggy Mountain Banjo," which I have seen reissued as LE 10043. There were also some worthy reissues on Columbia's Harmony budget label, and most of these are worth picking up. The two "live" LPs (one from Carnegie Hall, the other from Vanderbilt University) are both excellent, but the band's sound was beginning to soften as these were released. The late 1960s material ranges from pleasant to painful, and I advise you to listen to the albums before buying them. They aren't exactly bluegrass.

The Earl Scruggs Review still records for Columbia, and their recent albums feature some really great instrumental work by Earl, Randy Scruggs, Buck Graves, Vassar Clements, and others. They aren't exactly bluegrass either, but they're often very exciting.

Lester Flatt records for RCA and, like Scruggs, his records are generally available "on the racks." Instrumentally, they are still able to cut it, but the vocals are not the biting stuff of twenty-five years ago. The three duet albums with Mac Wiseman are quite listenable and even made the charts.

The Stanley Brothers

The very active Ralph Stanley International Fan Club, headed by Fay McGinnis, often claims that the Stanley Brothers were the most-recorded bluegrass-style band. This may well be true, although I'm not sure that anyone has ever been able to keep an accurate account of all the little labels they recorded for in their long career.

They were, of course, among the very earliest bands to record in the bluegrass style back in the mid-1940s, and I have an album on the Melodeon label that attests to this. It's called "The Stanley Brothers: Their Original Recordings," and it is actually several cuts from their very early Rich-R-Tone material.

The Stanleys joined the ranks of major-label bluegrass in the late 1940s, and the memorable occasion has been captured on two Harmony LPs, "The Stanley Brothers" (HL 7291) and "The Angels Are Singing" (HS 11177). Both are exquisite, although I'm not sure if they are available at this writing. They both include some of those hair-raising trios with Carter, Ralph, and Pee Wee Lambert.

The fabulous Stanley Mercury material has never been properly represented on American long-play releases. There have been one or two, and the most common that I've seen in the "cheapie" bins is one titled "Hard Times" (SR 60884). It includes some of the best and some that aren't so great, like the semi-boogie-woogie "So Blue." Still, the title tune is a solid Ralph Stanley banjo piece that is worth the price of the LP.

The Stanley Brothers' stay with Starday records was not a long one, but they turned out some really fine music. An album I've seen occasionally on the racks for under a dollar was one released on the Nashville sublabel and titled "Mountain Song Favorites" (NLP 2014). It's great.

Cincinnati's King Records were never ones to skimp on the releases, and their bands were, if anything, overrecorded. This was true of the Stanley Brothers also. Some of their King releases were great, others were not, and the great quantity of their King material makes it very hard to narrow it down to one or two "best." Their first King album (615) was great in every respect. It's worth going out of your way to find. The same may be said of King 645, which features their gospel sound at its best. Both are recommended. There is one other King LP that I recommend: King 872. It's all instrumental (Ralph and lead guitarist George Shuffler) and it's the largest dose of the Ralph Stanley mountain-style banjo found anywhere—on any LP. Don't be discouraged by its unappealing title, "America's Finest Five-String Banjo Hootenanny"!

Carter died while the brothers were still with King, and Ralph did one or two more for them on his own, with Larry Sparks, as well as some recordings for the smaller labels like Jalyn and Michigan Bluegrass. He is now with Rebel Records, and his Rebel material so far has been superb, as good or better than anything he and Carter recorded together.

Jimmy Martin

It's very easy to give a blanket recommendation for the recorded work of Jimmy Martin and the Sunny Mountain Boys. I have personal favorites, but the general sound and quality of all his MCA (Decca) releases are about the same. Don't be afraid to pick up any one you see in the record store. It'll have drive, bounce, sock, punch, and any other of the adjectives that apply to Jimmy and his band. My favorites are "Good 'n' Country" (DL 4016) and "This World Is Not My Home" (DL 74360).

But beware the novelty tune. Unless it's an instrumental or religious album, it'll be riddled with those silly ditties like "Goin' Ape" and "The Old Man's Drunk Again." Try to put performance over material, though, and you won't have any trouble.

There have been one or two sporadic releases of the material recorded with Bob Osborne (1951) and the Osborne Brothers (1954), but the most readily available at this time is the RCA "Vintage" LP "Early Bluegrass" (LPV–569). Not everything on the LP really qualifies as bluegrass, but Jimmy and the Osborne Brothers do a splendid job on "Chalk Up Another One," "Save It! Save It!" and the classic "20/20 Vision."

There is also the Nitty Gritty Dirt Band's "Will the Circle Be Unbroken?" album, and Jimmy was in truly great form for that session.

Don Reno and Red Smiley

Most of the Reno and Smiley work was for King, but their general quality through the hundreds of songs they recorded for the Cincinnati-based label seems to be generally higher than that of the Stanleys.

Again, it's hard to pick favorites, and not everything is still available. The only Reno and Smiley LP I've heard and didn't like was their Civil War LP, which consisted of recitations. For a real crush of the great Don Reno and his banjo, try to find King 552 and King 787. Both are instrumental LPs, separated by a few years, and Reno's work is often unbelievable. Again, if you can find them, try getting King 579 and 848 for a taste of the great duet singing. And there's also that classic 550, the gospel LP that started their career.

Jim and Jesse

We can't make a blanket recommendation on the recorded work of the McReynolds Brothers, which has drifted between bluegrass and "straight" country music since the mid-1960s.

There have been reports that their very early recordings as the Virginia Trio are still to be found on the Palace label. These, of course, have no banjo, but the singing is really nice in spite of the generally poor quality of Palace records. They are pressed on the cheapest vinyl and are severely overechoed and crudely rechanneled to simulate a stereo sound.

APPENDIX

A few years ago Capitol reissued their fabulous early 1950s Jim and Jesse material in a beautiful, budget-priced double album, "Twenty Great Songs" (DTBB-264). It went out of print almost immediately, but it was a phenomenally good record, and I consider it almost indispensable.

The Starday material (late 1950s) has never been pushed on the long-play market, which is a shame. There is more than enough of their Starday work to comprise an LP, and if packaged right, it would be a project well worth the effort. This was the band that included Bobby Thompson and Vassar Clements.

Epic did a beautiful job of producing their Jim and Jesse records, but these are becoming rare, since the brothers no longer record for Epic. Still, their "Bluegrass Special," "Bluegrass Classics," "Y'all Come," and Epic gospel material is worth looking for.

The McReynolds Brothers have found it wise to limit their bluegrass recording to a small label called Prize Records, and they sell these at their appearances. In terms of quality, they are as good as anything they have ever recorded.

The Osborne Brothers

Unfortunately, most of the classic Osborne Brothers material is unavailable. Bob Osborne's work with the Lonesome Pine Fiddlers has long been buried, as has his work with Jimmy Martin. Sonny Osborne has done a little better, having been present at the sessions that produced some of the most widely circulated Bill Monroe material.

The songs they recorded circa 1953 for Gateway may occasionally be seen in the 99¢ rack under the name Stanley Alpine. If you see that name (often on the Palace label), buy the record. They're not the best ever recorded, but they certainly are interesting.

The only widely circulated material from their days with Jimmy Martin is on the RCA "Vintage" album.

It's a shame that so little has been released from their great MGM days. Some of the MGM material was shallow, some of it had electric instruments, but it was all interesting and well performed. One album that may still be found on a dusty shelf somewhere was reissued on the MGM Golden Archive Series, "The Osborne Brothers" (Gas-140). Again, not all of it is "heavy," but it does include a few cuts from the days with Red Allen, including the classic "Once More."

153

The Osborne's have been with MCA (Decca) for about ten years. They've gotten progressively "Nashville" with each release, but their trio is still sublime. There's always good banjo and mandolin, but now it's mixed in with electric guitars and pianos.

We have been talking only of the major bands. There are dozens of others, and dozens of labels.

The Country Gentlemen, the Seldom Scene, Ralph Stanley, the Shenandoah Cut-Ups, and the Country Store all have records out on the very important Rebel label, even though the Country Gentlemen now record for Vanguard.

County Records has long been one of the champions of recording the best of the lesser-knowns, as well as reissuing a lot of the great old-time material from the 1920s. Among the fine bluegrass bands with records on County are the Lilly Brothers, Red Allen, Curtis Blackwell and Randall Collins, Mac Martin, and Larry Richardson. Also on this label are fine fiddle recordings by the great Kenny Baker.

Rounder Records, from Somerville, Massachusetts, has been producing fine music on its label for the past few years, including performances by Frank Wakefield, Don Stover, Joe Val and the New England Bluegrass Boys, Snuffy Jenkins and Pappy Sherril, the Blue Sky Boys, and Country Cooking.

Rome Records has the II Generation. Lemco was responsible for the great J. D. Crowe output of a few years back. Revonah is an upstate New York label that still specializes in straight, old-time bluegrass, as heard on their recent Shenandoah Cut-Ups releases.

Carl Story has made the rounds on the smaller labels, and his sound is the same now as it was twenty years ago, his incredible falsetto voice still intact.

Mac Wiseman's best bluegrass work was for Dot many years ago. A best bet is that old "'Tis Sweet to Be Remembered" LP, if you can still find it. A more recent offering (though also probably unavailable) was the LP titled "Bluegrass," on which Mac was joined by two other rotund pickers, Bob and Sonny Osborne. Both records will be very difficult to find.

APPENDIX

MAGAZINES

Bluegrass Unlimited

This fine magazine was founded in the Washington, D.C., area in 1966. Then, it was a few legal-sized, mimeographed pages stapled together at the upper left-hand corner.

We saw it progress into a small, black-and-white offset booklet (two staples), then to it's present glossy-cover form, all in eight years.

The *BU* staff is comprised of long-time bluegrass people, proving again that when something good happens to bluegrass, it almost always comes from within. The editor is Pete Kuykendall, a banjoist formerly with both Red Allen and the Country Gentlemen.

Bluegrass Unlimited covers the wide range of bluegrass thought and activity. Queries are answered, festivals announced, current records reviewed, banjo gadgets sold, Martin guitars advertised. *Bluegrass Unlimited* is just about indispensable for those with a genuine interest in the field (Monthly; $6.00 per year; Box 111, Broad Run, Virginia 22014)

Muleskinner News

Muleskinner is much along the same lines as *Bluegrass Unlimited* in terms of general concept, though pains are taken to do original things within the established format. This magazine was founded in 1969 as the house organ for the Carlton Haney Festival Organization, but Haney has actually had little to do with it. Editorial chores were handled by a young Virginian-at-Harvard named Fred Bartenstein, who did an outstanding job of making the magazine work.

If *Muleskinner News* has an edge over *Bluegrass Unlimited* (and comparisons are always being made), it is in the old picture department. Some of the faded oldies the *Muleskinner* staff comes up with are incredible.

The *Muleskinner* record reviews have been accused of being noncommital (*Bluegrass Unlimited*'s were once noted for being very harsh), but they are perceptively well-written. (Monthly; $7.00 per year; Rte. 2, Box 304, Elon College, North Carolina 27244)

APPENDIX

Pickin'

This is a relatively new publication on the scene. The editor-in-chief is New York bluegrass organizer Doug Tuchman. It features well-written articles on artists and instruments, but the strong suit of *Pickin'* is its handsome production job and beautiful color photography. Where else could one find a full-color, centerfold poster of Bill Monroe? (Monthly; $6.00 per year; 1 Saddle Road, Cedar Knolls, New Jersey 07927)

Other Bluegrass Publications*

American Old-Time Fiddler's News
6141 Morrill Ave.
Lincoln, Neb. 68507

Banjo Newsletter
1310 Hawkins La.
Annapolis, Md. 21401
monthly—$6.00 per year

Bluegrass Central
Box 162
Stillwater, Okla. 74074
monthly—$5.00 per year

Blue Grass Reflections
Southwest Blue Grass Club
P.O. Box 117
Coppell, Tx. 75019
monthly—$5.00 per year

Blue Grass Special
3047 N. Brighton
Rosemead, Ca. 91770

Blue Grass Strings
South Florida Blue Grass Association
8400 S.W. 92nd Street
Miami, Fla. 33156

Country Music
P.O. Box 2560
Boulder, Col. 80302
monthly—$7.00 per year

County Sales Newsletter
P.O. Box 191
Floyd, Va. 24091
free to customers

Devil's Box
Tennessee Valley Old Time Fiddlers
  Association
Rte. 4
Madison, Ala. 35758
quarterly—$3.00 per year

Disc Collector Newsletter
P.O. Box 169
Cheswold, Del. 19936
11 issues—$2.00

Fiddle Faddle
Washington Old-Time Fiddlers
  Association
Box 225
Tenino, Wa. 98589

*Compiled with the assistance of *Muleskinner News*, Rte. 2, Box 304, Elon College, NC 27244

APPENDIX

Fiddler's News
Northeast Fiddlers Association
RFD#1
Stowe, Vt. 05672

Guitar Player
Box 615
Saratoga, Ca. 95070
monthly—$8.00 per year

The Hoedowner
150 N.W. 10th Street
Sherwood, Ore. 97140

Idaho Fiddler
3114 8th Street
Lewiston, Id. 83501

John Edwards Memorial Foundation
    Quarterly
Folklore and Mythology Center
University of California
Los Angeles, Ca. 90024
quarterly—$4.00 per year

Journal of Country Music
Country Music Foundation
700 16th Ave. So.
Nashville, Tn. 37203
quarterly

June Apple
P.O. Box 149
Shibuya
Tokyo 105-91, Japan

Mountain Music Shindig Tape Club
178 Vreeland Ave.
Rutherford, N.J. 07070
6 tapes—$3.00

Mugwumps Instrument Herald
12704-C Barbara Rd.
Silver Spring, Md. 20906
$5.00 per year

National Old Time Fiddlers Association
    Newsletter
716 Humboldt St.
Santa Rosa, Ca. 95404

Old-Time Music
33 Brunswick Gardens
London W8, England

Roundhouse Rag
P.O. Box 474
Somerville, Mass. 02144
free to customers

Sing Out!
106 W. 28th Street
New York, N.Y. 10001
bimonthly—$6.00 per year

Sound Post
California State Old Time Fiddler's
    Association
P.O. Box 1093
Oroville, Ca. 95965

Uncle Mike's Instrument Emporium
P.O. Box 267
Doylestown, Pa. 18901
free

Underground
1421 Gohier St.
St. Laurent Ville
Quebec, Canada

Voice from the Mountains
Southern Appalachian Musician's
    Co-op
1538 Highland Ave.
Knoxville, Tn. 37916

Washington Old Time Fiddler's
    Newsletter
789 North Jenifer La.
East Wenatchee, Wa. 98801

APPENDIX

*BLUEGRASS RADIO LISTING**

ARIZONA

Tucson—KWFM 92.9 FM
Chip Corry, DJ
"Blue Grass Express"
4–5 pm, Sat.

CALIFORNIA

Berkeley—KPFA 94.1 FM
Ray Edlund, DJ
"Pig in a Pen"
3–5:30 pm, every other Fri.

San Diego—KGB 1360 AM
                    101 FM
Old Brother Lou Curtiss, DJ
"Old Time Gospel Hour"
7 am, Sun.

Santa Cruz—KUSP 88.9 FM
Leigh Hill, DJ
"Pataphysical Farm and Poultry Show"
3–6 pm, Sun.

Genial John Simmons, DJ
"Road Apple Rodeo"

Santa Rosa—KURE 1460 AM
Tom Reed and the Homestead Act, DJ
"Blue Grass Jamboree"
1–4 pm, Sat.

COLORADO

Canon City—KCSP, closed circuit
Gary "Cotton" Adamson, DJ
"Meadow Muffin Special"
6:30–8 pm

Denver—KRML 98.5 FM
Mitch Levy, DJ
8–8:30 pm, daily, scattered

Denver—KCFR 91.2 FM
Pat Rossiter, DJ
"Bluegrass Breakdown"
10–11:30 am, Sat.

WASHINGTON, D.C.

WAMU 88.5 FM
Gary Henderson and Katy Daley, DJs
"This Is Bluegrass. . ."
8 am–12 noon, Sat.
"Stained-Glass Bluegrass"
9–11 am, Sun.

FLORIDA

Sarasota—WQSA 1220 AM
                    WQSR 102.5 FM
Tom Henderson, DJ
"This Is Blue Grass"
3 pm, Sat. (syndicated)

*Compiled with the assistance of *Muleskinner News,* Rte. 2, Box 304, Elon College, NC 27244.

Tampa—WHBO 1050 AM
Tom Henderson, DJ
"This Is Blue Grass"
1 pm, Sun. (syndicated)

GEORGIA

Atlanta—WRFG 89.3 FM
Larry Lee, DJ
"Bluegrass Festival"
8–9 pm, Wed.
7–8 pm, Sat.

Buford—WGCO 102 FM
Rev. Jim Whitlock, DJ
"Gospel Bluegrass"
1–3:30 pm, Mon.-Fri.

Buford—WGCO 102 FM
          WDYZ AM
Chuck Bagley, DJ
scattered bluegrass
3:30–7 pm, Mon.-Fri.

Thomasville—WLOR 730 AM
Tom Henderson, DJ
"This Is Blue Grass"
2 pm, Sun. (syndicated)
also scattered bluegrass

ILLINOIS

Champaign—WTWC 103.9 FM
Bill Taylor, DJ
"Farmer Bill Blue Grass Show"
8–9 pm, Sat.

Chicago—WJJD 104.3 FM
Mark Edwards, DJ
"Bluegrass Special"
11–12 pm, Sat.

Galesburg—WAAG 94.9 FM
Denny Shaw, Ralph Schoen, John
   Biermann, DJs
bluegrass mixed with regular country
   format
all day

INDIANA

Scottsburg—WMPI 100.9 FM
George Stephens, DJ
11 am–12 noon, Sat.

IOWA

Iowa City—WSUI AM
             KSUI FM
John Monick, Music Director
scattered bluegrass

KANSAS

Lawrence—KANU 91.5 FM
William Evans, DJ
"Bluegrass and Old Time Music"
7–8 pm, Sat.

KENTUCKY

Ashland—WTCR 1420 AM
Jim Forbes, DJ
scattered bluegrass

Bowling Green—WLBJ 1410 AM
                      WLBJ 96.7 FM
Don Pierson, DJ
3–6 pm, Sun.

APPENDIX

MAINE

Portland—WPOR
scattered bluegrass

MARYLAND

Baltimore—WBJC 91.5 FM
Carlton Robinette, DJ
"Folk Roots"
12 noon–1 pm, Tue.

Frostburg—WFRB 560 AM
WFRB 105.3 FM
Ted Evans, Music Director
scattered bluegrass

Havre de Grace—WASA 1330 AM
WHDG 103.7 FM
Jason Pate and Don Matsen, DJs
"Jason Pate Show"
"Country 103"

Westminster—WTTR
6–6:30 am

MASSACHUSETTS

Boston—WCOP 1150 AM
Don Thomas, DJ
scattered bluegrass

Cambridge—WCAS 740 AM
12–4 pm, Sun. (live broadcast)
folk, old-time, and bluegrass

Cambridge—WHRB 95.3 FM
Brian Sinclair, Dave Schmaltz, DJs
"Hillbilly at Harvard"
10 am–1 pm, Sat.

Cambridge—WTBS 88.1 FM
The Rounders, DJs
"Give the Fiddler a Dram"
5–7 pm, Wed.

Fitchburg—WFGL 104.5 FM
Patty Ann Hollins, DJ
4–5 pm, Wed.

Lynn—WLYN 101.7 FM
Glen Shields, DJ
10–11 pm, Mon.–Fri.

Medford—WMFO 90.1 FM
"Rounder Collective"
6–8 pm, Wed.

Waltham—WBRS 91.7 FM
Don Weber, DJ
"The Orange Blossom Special"
6–8 pm, Sun.

MICHIGAN

Ann Arbor—WNRS 1290 AM
WNRZ 103 FM
John Morris, DJ
"The Blue Grass Show"
2–6 pm, Sat.

Detroit—WMUZ 103.5 FM
Fay McGinnis, DJ
"Mountain Echoes"
5:45 am, Mon.–Fri.
1:45 pm, Sat.

Ypsilanti—WYFC 1520 AM
John Morris, DJ
"Blue Grass Gospeltime"
8–9 am, Sat.

160

APPENDIX

MISSOURI

Columbia—KBIA 91.3 FM
4 pm, Sun.

Columbia—KOPN 89.7 FM
Thomas Schierman, Jr., and Joe Zanda,
  DJs
"The Blue Grass and Old-Time Music
  Show"
10 am–12 noon, Sat.
"Blue Grass Music 'Live' Parachute
  Room"
6:30–7:30 pm, Sun.
"Old-Time Fiddling"
4:30–5:30 pm, Tues.
"Mid Week Pick Up"
4–5 pm, Thurs.

Houston—KBTC 1250 AM
Walt Lawson, DJ
"Old Time Blue Grass"
6:40 am, daily

Kansas City—KBIL 1140 AM
Mike O'Roark, DJ
"Proud Country Bluegrass Hour"
6:30 pm, Sat.

Rolla—KUMR 88.5 FM
Mike Morgan, DJ
"Bluegrass"
8–10 pm, Sat.

St. Louis—KWMU 90.7 FM
Jeff Cook, DJ
7:15 pm, Sun.

St. Louis—KWRE 730 AM
Jeff Cook, DJ
"Blue Grass Express"
12 noon, Sat.

Warrensburg—KOKO 1450 AM
Herman Smith, DJ
11:05 pm–12 noon, Sat.

NEW HAMPSHIRE

Claremont—WECM 106.1 FM
           WTSY 1230 AM
Jerry Fox, DJ
"Country Music"
6 am–12 noon, Sat.

NEW YORK

Liverpool [Syracuse]—WCNY 91.3 FM
Bill Knowlton, DJ
"Blue Grass Ramble"
10 pm–1 am, Sun.

New York—WBAI 99.5 FM
Tom Whitmore, DJ
"Grassroots of Music"
4 pm, Fri.
8 pm, Sat.

NORTH CAROLINA

Farmville—WFAG 1250 AM
Tom Henderson, DJ
"Bluegrass USA"
2 pm, Sat. (syndicated)

Henderson—WXNC 92.5 FM
Tom Henderson, DJ
"This Is Blue Grass"
10 pm, Fri. (syndicated)

King—WKTE 1090 AM
Chuck Webster, DJ
"Blue Grass Hoedown"
1–5 pm, Sat.

Mooresville—WHIP 1350 AM
Hilda McAlpine, DJ
6–9 am, Mon.-Sat.

Wilmington—WECT (TV Channel 6)
"Red White Snow"
bluegrass gospel
9–9:30 am, Sun.

OHIO

Columbus—WOSR
Larry Nager, DJ
"Bluegrass and New Grass"
12–3 am, Sun.

Middletown—WPFB 910 AM
Moon Mullins, DJ
"Moon Mullins Show"
5–7 am, and 3–5:30 pm

Yellow Springs—WYSO FM
Jim Lewis, DJ
1–3 pm, Mon.

OKLAHOMA

Eufaula—KCES 102.3 FM
Clark Davis and Jim Mitchell, DJs
7:30–8 pm, daily plus
  occasional tunes throughout the day

Stillwater—KOSV 91.7 FM
Prof. George Carney, DJ
"Blue Grass Review"
7–7:30 pm, Sat.

Tulsa—KTUL (TV Channel 8)
"John Chick Show"
7–8 pm, Fri.

OREGON

Corvallis—KLOO 1430 AM
        KLOO 106.1 FM
B. J. Johnson, DJ
Sawtooth Mountain Boys, live
"Home Comfort Blue Grass Music
  Time"
9:30 pm, Mon.

PENNSYLVANIA

Boyertown—WBYO 107.5 FM
James Snavely, Wilmer Borneman, DJs
"Milk Bucket Serenade"
"Country Caravan"

Ephrata—WIOV 105.1 FM
Bobby "The Ole Sheriff" Montgomery,
  DJ
6–8 pm, daily

Erie—WQLN 91.3 FM
Harold Libell (Hal Lee), DJ
"Blue Grass Session"
3–5 pm, Sun.

Pittsburgh—WDUQ 90.5 FM
Mark Yacovone, DJ
"Blue Grass Special"
7–8 pm, Thursday

Red Lion—WGCB 1440 AM
Bill Runkle, DJ
3–4 pm, Sat.

Warren—WRRN 92.3 FM
Dave Engstrom and Diana Jarrell, DJs
"Bluegrass Express"
4–5 pm, Sun.

APPENDIX

SOUTH CAROLINA

Greenville—WESC
Wally Mullinax, DJ

TENNESSEE

Collierville—WMSO 1590 AM
Jack Mayes, DJ
"Blue Grass Country"
8–10 am, Sat.

Knoxville—WVOT 91.9 FM
Paul Campbell, DJ
"Music of the Southern Mountains"
7:30, Tues.

Mountain City—WMCT 1390 AM
Carl Story, DJ
6–10 am, daily

Nashville—WRVU 91.1 FM
Tom Henderson, DJ
"This Is Blue Grass"
10:30 pm, Wed. (syndicated)

Warrenton—WKCW 1420 AM
"Sunday Breakdown"
3–3:30 pm
"Blue Grass Startime"
2–2:30 pm, Sat.
substantial daily programming

TEXAS

San Angelo—KPEP
James Pinkston, DJ
every hour on the half hour

UTAH

Murray—KMOR 1230 AM
Jay Meehan, DJ
"Mellow Country"
midnight–6 am

VIRGINIA

Abingdon—WBBI 1230 AM
WBBI 92.7 FM
Bob Jones and Lee Harmon, DJs
"Best in Bluegrass"
6:30–10 pm, Mon.

Altavista—WKDE AM/FM
Les Woodie, DJ
6–7 am, Sat.
plus scattered bluegrass

Bristol—WZAP 690 AM
(Formerly WCYB)
"Farm and Fun Time"
12 noon–2 pm

Farmville—WFLO 870 AM
WFLO 95.7 FM
Henry M. Fulcher, DJ
FM: 5–6:30 am, Mon.-Sat.
7–10 pm, Sun.
AM: 5–9 am, 10 am–1 pm, Mon.–Sat

Hampton—WTID
Mike Allen, DJ
1–2 pm, Sat.

Pulaski—WBLB 1510 AM
Harold Hill, DJ
"Blue Grass Time"
5–6 pm, daily

Roanoke—WVWR 90.1 FM
Mike Haynie, DJ
"Bluegrass Revue"
9 pm, Sun.

Rocky Mount—WYTI 1570 AM
Bill Vernon, DJ
"Blue Grass Special"
1-2 pm, Mon.-Fri.

Stuart—WHEO 1270 AM
Sam Bass, DJ
"Blue Grass Roundup"
10 am–12 noon, Sat.

WEST VIRGINIA

Ravenswood—WMOV 1360 AM
D. Hoyt, DJ
"Open Road Show"
1-4 pm, Mon.-Fri.

CANADA AND ABROAD

Quebec, Canada—CKRL 89.1 FM
Hubert Tremblay, DJ
"Saute, crapaud"
7 pm, Wed.

Cornwall, Ontario, Canada—CJSS 1220
　AM
Keith Clingen, DJ

Sault Ste. Marie, Ontario,
　Canada—CJIC
Don Ramsay, DJ

Sussex, England—BBC Radio Brighton
Jim Marshall, DJ
6:15 pm, Tues.

BLUEGRASS AND RELATED ORGANIZATIONS*

Allegheney Blue Grass Club
Betty Raines
Short Gap, W. Va.

American Old Time Fiddler's
  Association
Delores DeRyke
6141 Morrill Ave.
Lincoln, Neb. 68507

Appalachian Fiddle and Blue Grass
  Association
Ralph T. Unroe
225 Park Ave.
Milton, Pa. 17847

Blue Grass Club of Japan
Katsuhiko Usami
188 Wada Michi
Hodogaya Ku, Yokohama 240
Japan

Blue Grass Club of New York
Douglas Tuchman
417 E. 89th St.
New York, N.Y. 10028

Blue Grass Society of the Ozarks
MPO Box 965
Springfield, Mo. 65801

Boston Area Friends of Blue Grass and
  Old-Time Country Music
Nancy Talbott
238 Putman Ave.
Cambridge, Ma. 02139

California State Oldtime Fiddlers
  Association
P.O. Box 1093
Oroville, Ca. 95965

Carter Family Fan Club
Dot and Bob Patton
2802 Fortland Dr.
Nashville, Tn. 37206

Colorado Bluegrass Society
Michael Williams
1040 Cedar St.
Broomfield, Co. 80020

Country Gentlemen Fan Club
Yvonne Lloyd
Box 387
Hagerstown, Md. 21740

Country Music Association
1511 Sigler St.
Nashville, Tn. 37203

Country Music Foundation
700 16th Ave. So.
Nashville, Tn. 37203

Eddie and the Mueller Brothers Fan Club
Rose Baley
325 E. Cavanaugh
Lansing, Mi. 48910

John Edwards Memorial Foundation
Folklore and Mythology Center
University of California
Los Angeles, Ca. 90024

*Compiled with the assistance of *Muleskinner News,* Rte. 2, Box 304, Elon College,
NC 27244.

APPENDIX

Betty Fisher Fan Club
Marie M. Boykin
2466 Savannah Hwy.
Charleston, N.C. 29407

Florida Friends of Bluegrass Society
Tom Henderson
7318 Sequoia Dr.
Tampa, Fla. 33617

Indiana Friends of Bluegrass
Ron Nolan
8302 Geffs Dr.
Indianapolis, Ind. 46239

Jim and Jesse Fan Club
Jean S. Osborn
404 Shoreline Dr.
Tallahassee, Fla. 32301

Kansas Blue Grass Association
Jean Duncan, Secretary
2781 Hiram
Wichita, Ks. 67217

Lewis Family Fan Club
Thelda Owens
Rte. 2, Box 121
Junction City, Ark. 71749

Jimmy Martin Fan Club
Mary Ann Garrison
P.O. Box 46
Hermitage, Tn. 37076

Missouri Area Blue Grass Committee
220 St. Mary's
Bethalto, Ill. 62010

Bill Monroe International Fan Club
Glen Mowery
Rte. 3, Box 219
Claremore, Okla. 74017

James Monroe Fan Club
Mary Ruth Stamey
Rte. 2, Box 685
Brevard, N.C. 28712

Charlie Moore Fan Club
Carol Dickerson
5750 Leland Dr.
Ann Arbor, Mi. 48105

Olkahoma Blue Grass Club
Box 642
Shawnee, Okla. 74801

Oldtime Country Music Club of Canada
Bob Fuller
1421 Gohier St.
Ville St. Laurent, Quebec, Canada

Pine Tree State Blue Grass Music
    Association
Jimmy Cox
4 Garden Lane
Topsham, Me. 04086

Portland Banjo and Fiddle Club
Julie Joel, Secretary
4133 S.W. Corbett St., Apt. 2
Portland, Ore. 97201

Roanoke Fiddle and Banjo Club
Mrs. Margaret Worrell
304 Union Street
Salem, Va. 24153

Society for the Preservation of Blue
    Grass Music of America
Chuck Stearnman
4017 Bell
Kansas City, Mo. 64111

South Florida Blue Grass Association
8400 SW 92nd Street
Miami, Fla. 33156

APPENDIX

Southern Appalachian Musician's
Co-op
1538 Highland Ave.
Knoxville, Tn. 37916

Southside Virginia Blue Grass
Association
Paul Bock
3711 Westwood Dr.
Petersburg, Va. 23803

Southwest Blue Grass Club
P.O. Box 117
Coppell, Tx. 75019

Larry Sparks Fan Club
Greta Stewart
2704 Haley Ave.
Ft. Worth, Tx. 76117

Ralph Stanley International Fan Club
Fay McGinnis
1156 21st Street
Wyandotte, Mi. 48192

Carl Story Fan Club
Ron Wiggins
Rte. 5, McLains
Newton, Ks. 67114

Tennessee Valley Old Time Fiddler's
Association
Rte. 4
Madison, Ala. 35758

Texas Blue Grass Association
Lee Bridgewater
6544 Baker Blvd.
Ft. Worth, Tx. 76118

Toronto Area Bluegrass Club
60 Ruddington Drive, Apt. 1307
Willowdale, Ont., Canada M2K 2J9

Tulsa Blue Grass Association
Box 1242
Tulsa, Okla. 74101

Western Pennsylvania Blue Grass
Committee
P.O. Box 10223
Pittsburgh, Pa. 15232

West Virginia Blue Grass Association
Jimmy Nicholas
2 So. Stonewall Street
Sutton, W. Va. 26601

Chubby Wise Fan Club
Helen Cline
7208 Karen Drive
Ft. Worth, Tx. 76118

Bibliography

Most of the information in this book came from sources other than the many books available on country music. Almost all of the published serious writing on the subject of bluegrass has appeared either in magazines like *Bluegrass Unlimited* and *Muleskinner News* or the more scholarly quarterly of the John Edwards Memorial Foundation. Serious students of bluegrass music should read all back issues of these publications, as most of what I've written came from them, as well as scattered works such as Mayne Smith's important master's thesis on bluegrass; some of the great work being done by Neil V. Rosenberg at the Memorial University of Newfoundland; the research of the Country Music Foundation's Doug Green; and the work of Smithsonian's Ralph Rinzler. Another good source is *Disc Collector* magazine, in issues far too numerous to mention. One of the beautiful features of *Disc Collector* has always been the extensive discographical information of many of the greats of old-time music and bluegrass. The following is a list of books related to or containing information about bluegrass or its roots. In most cases, much text has to be waded through to find reference to the specific style of bluegrass.

Child, James Francis. *English and Scottish Popular Ballads*. Boston: Houghton Mifflin Co., 1965. (10 volumes, 1882-1898). Child collected British ballads in the southern mountains, many of which were in purer form in Appalachia than in England.

Cohen, John, and Seeger, Mike. *The New Lost City Ramblers Song Book*. New York: Oak Publications. A collection of the songs recorded for the major record companies by rural artists from the early 1920s through the late 1940s, with excellent background on old-time music and bluegrass.

BIBLIOGRAPHY

Emerson, Bill. "On the Road with Jimmy Martin," in *Bluegrass Unlimited*. Vol. 3 No. 4, October 1968.

Gentry, Linnell. *History and Encyclopedia of Country, Western, and Gospel Music*. Nashville: McQuiddy Press, 1961.

Malone, Bill C. *Country Music U.S.A.* Austin, Texas: University of Texas Press, 1974. Possibly the best work written on country music.

Moore, Thurston. *Country Music Who's Who*. Denver: Heather Publications.

Rooney, James. *Bossmen: Bill Monroe and Muddy Waters*. New York: The Dial Press, 1971.

Scruggs, Earl. *Earl Scruggs and the Five-String Banjo*. Nashville, Tenn.: Peer International. An instruction manual with much information on the man and his style.

Sharp, Cecil J. *English Folk Songs from the Southern Appalachians*. London: Oxford University Press, 1932. Sharp, like Child, was primarily concerned with finding examples of British ballads in the South.

Shelton, Robert, and Goldblatt, Burt. *The Country Music Story*. Secaucus, N.J.: Castle Books, 1966.

Stambler, Irwin, and Landon, Grelun. *Encyclopedia of Folk, Country, and Western Music*. New York: St. Martin's Press, 1969.

Index

171

INDEX